CON

M000106626

FOREWORD

I've always been a fan of international football.

Throughout my whole coaching career, I've wanted my players to represent their country. They become better players through this experience. Playing for your nation should be something every rugby league player should aspire to do.

When the New Zealand Rugby League approached me to help with their World Cup preparations in 2008, I initially said no. I didn't feel I was the right person to be the head coach. I thought the Kiwis needed a New Zealander in charge, and Stephen Kearney was a proud Kiwi and a very talented coach. I was happy to assist in the background and help with preparation. Once that was confirmed, I was excited about the challenge.

Being involved with New Zealand in the 2008 World Cup tournament was one of the most satisfying moments of my career. I knew that they had wonderful talent, but perhaps not always the belief needed to achieve the ultimate outcome. I felt that if I helped improve them in this area then they had every change of winning the World Cup.

When Nathan Cayless held the World Cup trophy up high after the final, I was immensely proud. I had made a contribution to the team. I was proud of the way both teams played in the final. It was a great test match – tough, physically demanding and skillful.

The 2008 World Cup really displayed how good international football could be. In particular, I was really impressed by the Pacific island teams, like Samoa, Tonga and Fiji.

My motivations were the same when England approached me. I've had a long-standing interest in seeing England do well.

England has been strong previously but a stronger England is wonderful for the international game. I remember watching the Great Britain teams of the 1960s and 1970s. Their clashes with Australia were always something I enjoyed watching. It was good, tough football, full of emotion.

I'm looking forward to working with the England team again and hopefully making a good contribution this summer. International football has come a long way in the last decade. I've got high hopes for well-supported 2017 World Cup here in Australia, New Zealand and Papua New Guinea.

Andrew's book really brings to life the spirit and pride of representing your country. I encourage all rugby league fans to have a read and relive the great moments throughout World Cup history.

Wayne Bennett
Brisbane, April 2017

INTRODUCTION

I returned to my seat in the front row of Brisbane's Suncorp Stadium and admired my dinner: a tightly wrapped steak and cheese pie, a small box of skin-burning hot chips and a cold, 600 ml bottle of Coca-Cola. It wasn't gourmet food by any stretch, but it still set me back a total of $18.50. I began to open a very small square of tomato sauce and promptly drowned the hot potato items in the thin red liquid. The chips had no chance.

As I counted the meagre change left from my $20 note, I looked up to see some of Australia's greatest players making their way around the ground. To mark the country's one hundredth year of rugby league, the 'team of the century' was named and included the likes of Bob Fulton, Mal Meninga, Wally Lewis and Andrew Johns, who were now waving to the cheering spectators.

It was quite a moment: Australia's previous rugby league greats were now passing the mantle to the current team, who were about to finish preparations for the 2008 final, a game that would shake international rugby league to its foundations.

And the sport needed it. Yes, rugby league is second oldest only to soccer in the World Cup stakes, but a mixture of formats and irregular cycles had blunted its impact on regular rugby league fans. These issues and Australia's relative dominance hasn't meant that the tournaments have lacked for entertainment or close contests, though.

Ever since France had the courage to host the first event in 1954, through to the magnificent recent incarnation in 2013, we've seen many games that have left indelible memories for all who witnessed them. We've had teams stage amazing comebacks under siege, such as the 1954 French and Great Britain sides or the 2008 Kiwi team. There have been referee controversies, such as those that marred the 1970 and 1972 finals. Internal politics have always raged: the 1988 Australians had to shake off a huge interstate mess only a few years earlier plus 1995's ARL v. Super League war. We've also enjoyed the underdog throwing the odd sucker punch, like the brilliant Clive Griffith-coached Welsh teams and the United States' spirited run in 2013, among others.

I've chosen ten stand-out matches from over sixty years of World Cup history, and attempted to bring them to life and tell their stories. From France's dazzling early performances, Britain's dramatic 1970 victory through to more modern-day classics like Lewis's 1988 Australians, the 1995 semi-final between the Kiwis and Kangaroos and England's epic semi against New Zealand, this book recalls the big plays and talks to those players, coaches and referees involved in some of the sport's biggest moments.

The price of a stadium dinner might have gone up –
as well as the quality of the food – but the entertainment
and colour of rugby league World Cups have continued
to inspire. I hold high hopes for the upcoming 2017 event
in Australasia and Papua New Guinea. I hope you enjoy
reading and reliving the great characters, coaches and
controversies retold in these pages.

Match 1, 1954

A 'TIN POT COMPETITION' IS BORN

France v. Great Britain

Parc des Princes, Paris, France
13 November 1954
World Cup final

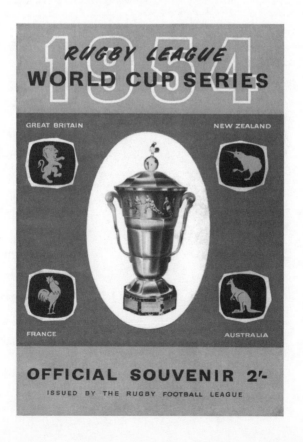

FRANCE	GREAT BRITAIN
1. Robert Puig Aubert (captain)	1. Jim Ledgard
2. Vincent Cantoni	2. David Rose
3. Claude Teisseire	3. Phil Jackson
4. Jacques Merquey	4. Albert Naughton
5. Raymond Contrastin	5. Mick Sullivan
6. Antoine Jiminez	6. Gordon Brown
7. Joseph Crespo	7. Gerry Helme
8. Joseph Krawzyk	8. John Thorley
9. Jean Audoubert	9. Sam Smith
10. Francois Rinaldi	10. Robert Coverdale
11. Armand Save	11. Basil Watts
12. Jean Pambrun	12. Don Robinson
13. Gilbert Verdier	13. David Valentine (captain)
Coach: Rene Duffort/Jean Duhau	Coach: Gideon Shaw

Referee: Charles Appleton

You could forgive Great Britain captain Dave Valentine for feeling a little uneasy. French fullback Robert Puig Aubert had just kicked a superb penalty goal to take the lead for his country. The score was 9–8 in favour of France, with half an hour to go in the first ever World Cup final.

On a sunny afternoon in Paris, the 30,368 mainly French fans were getting louder. Curiously, until that point, France hadn't looked like the team that had demolished the Kiwis 22–13 in pool play, or emerged victorious in a tough 15–5 defeat of Australia only two days earlier. But patches of typical French flair and some nerveless goal kicking from Puig Aubert meant France could enjoy a slender lead. The Parisian crowd could sense the match was turning.

Yet Valentine remained calm. A dour, hard-working player with a measured temperament, the Scotsman reorganised his troops under the cross bar for a few words of encouragement. There was no shouting, no demonstration, no panic. He and his team knew their roles. He simply reinforced the task ahead.

It was the British skipper's character traits – *Huddersfield Examiner* writer Sidney H. Crother also described him as tireless, whole-hearted and very modest – that served him so well as a dual international, firstly with Scotland in rugby union, then with Great Britain in rugby league. Valentine wasn't even the first choice captain for the World Cup tournament. Dickie Williams, Willie Horne and Ernest Ashcroft took turns at leading Great Britain's tours of Australia and New Zealand earlier in the year.

But the rugged and multi-skilled Valentine had such huge belief in himself and his team that nothing would be too tough to overcome. In between playing international rugby union and league, he also tried his hand successfully at professional wrestling. Great Britain was in good hands, and his teammates knew it.

Halfback Gerry Helme later remarked that he 'had all the confidence in the world under Davy's captaincy'.

Yet no other rookie captain in rugby league's international history faced as much adversity as he did. He had effectively turned a rabble of a team, plagued by withdrawals, injuries and boycotts, into a powerhouse, big on team spirit.

Valentine had to assume the role of captain, coach and trainer all in one. This campaign was as much about restoring pride both in the jersey and in the sport in Great Britain. At the same time, France's rise to the top of Test rugby league was a remarkable event in itself.

The French resistance

'Exhilarating in their football, unorthodox, spectacular, everything rugby league fans wanted to see.'

The French team certainly made an impression on their inaugural trip to Australia in 1951, as noted in the newsreel commentary at the time – yet these adjectives personified French rugby league for close to two decades.

It is incredible to think how far the side had developed in the previous decade considering rugby league had been banned in France in 1941. The young sporting upstart dared to pay its players and form professional competitions, a notion that wasn't aligned with the right-wing Vichy government's policy of asserting what it saw as traditional moral values. French sports minister Jean Borotra declared: 'Ligue Francaise de Rugby à XIII, is banned, its permit having been refused. The assets of the banned organisation … are transferred in their entirety to the National Sports Committee.'

The French Rugby League Federation suddenly had to give up everything: buildings, players, resources, coaches. All the League's revenue and profits were given to the National Sports Committee. Rugby league now had the status of the outlaw who was a dead man if he ever stepped back into town.

How did the French Rugby League Federation rise back from the depths of sporting poverty, fighting against its own national government, and reach the heights of hosting a world tournament?

The short answer: Paul Barrière, France's second and youngest French Rugby League president. After fighting with the French Resistance in World War II, when he met officials and key people in rugby league, he rose from club administrator to vice-president of the French body. Outgoing president Marcel Laborde, wanted to bring rugby league back to health and implored Barrière to step into action. It worked. From this moment, Barrière focused all his efforts into overturning this unprecedented government-sanctioned destruction of a sport.

Throughout 1945–47, rugby league was built up and restored in France. Barrière created more clubs, more competitions and brought a stream of rugby union players to the thirteen-a-side game. Through Puig Aubert's deeds, former players started to come back to league too.

In a huge coup, Barrière managed to get the sport recognised as an independent game in its own right in 1948. The French government accepted the re-entry of *jeu à XIII* ('the game of thirteen'; the word 'rugby' was still not allowed be used). It was only in 1968 that the name of the organisation was changed from 'The French Federation for the Game of 13' to 'The French Federation of Rugby 13'.

French rugby league historian Louis Bonnery summed it up best: Barrière's presidency brought the sport back to life in France and created a legacy that would remain long after he had left the president's chair. He flew the rugby league flag where others didn't and won over a rugby union-loving French sporting public.

A rugby league revolution

In the 1950s there was a genuine battle for international rugby league supremacy. All teams were evenly matched. Yet while Great Britain and Australia had the Ashes – a fiercely contested rivalry dating back to 1914 – France and New Zealand had to be satisfied with the occasional Test series.

France and Great Britain were the two most successful teams in the four-year lead-up to the World Cup, so it worked out extremely well for the International Rugby League Federation that they contested the final. The French had series wins against New Zealand and Australia, while the British defeated the Kiwis and France, but lost to the Kangaroos 3–0 in the Ashes in 1954.

Clive Churchill's Australians were wounded and hurting, despite thrashing Great Britain in that preceding series. They suffered defeats to France in 1952–53, plus the ignominy of a first series loss to New Zealand in 1953.

The Kiwis were rebuilding and introduced future greats like the Sorensen brothers into the tournament. They were probably fourth favourites going into the Cup, but still gave the French of 1951 a stern test, losing the series 1–2.

France was the new kid in town. The 1950s represented the golden years of rugby league in the country. They wowed their own crowds with their brand of *rugby à treize* – spirited, carefree, attacking football – and news of their deeds soon reached Australian shores. Barrière was able to secure a trip to Australia for a three-Test series that put the French team in the consciousness of every Australian who witnessed that amazing tour.

Playing a brand of sparkling, end-to-end football, with a host of enigmatic players and personalities, France signalled their intentions that they were no longer the junior at the rugby league table. They brought colour, vibrancy and fun to a sport in France that was still fighting hard for an identity. The local crowds swarmed to their team, with countless cartoons making Puig Aubert and his troops cult heroes.

Riding on this wave of enthusiasm and success on the world stage, Barrière was able to pitch a World Cup competition as a way to bring the rugby league world together. It also gave the four major nations a chance to play a series against each other.

A 'tin pot competition'

The World Cup tournament was officially set in motion. Barrière organised six host cities, with the final to be played at the Parc des Princes in Paris. There were to be three pool games and a final, with each team playing each other once. He also donated an eight million franc trophy and underwrote the tournament with the help of the French Rugby League.

In another coup, the BBC broadcasted the event to the whole of the United Kingdom via television – a first for sport in Europe, and a great fillip for the World Cup. British commentator Eddie Waring was a huge advocate of staging sporting events on television, having called rugby league matches on BBC radio throughout the previous decade. The World Cup was the first chance to test out the medium on a large audience.

Barrière felt this was the chance for international rugby league to shine in a tournament that would have long-lasting prestige. It also doubled as a celebration, marking twenty years since the formation of the French Rugby League Federation. The World Cup was his dream come true and the culmination of all those years of hard work and dedication. It should have been a straightforward process, right?

Unfortunately it wasn't. The other nations didn't share his enthusiasm.

For Australia and Britain, Barrière's proposal took away the lustre of their precious Ashes series. Both countries essentially thumbed their noses at Barrière and France through half-hearted commitment to the tournament when it was first announced. In some ways, it showed how insular the traditional world rugby league powers were at the time. In much more positive ways, it demonstrated Barrière's great vision at this early period of league history. He was a true pioneer.

The Australians were the first to go public and, gave a lukewarm response. *The Sydney Morning Herald* reported in 1953 that Australia would send a team. The sporting body hadn't committed yet though.

Great Britain had just returned from a taxing tour of Australasia. Players weren't interested in going. They were fatigued and not happy. Some players felt the £25 they would receive for touring was inadequate. Funding was in short supply also. Dave Valentine stepped into the vacant coaching role because they couldn't pay for a coach. Forget about a team photo too; too expensive.

Ray French, who played for Great Britain in 1968, felt the British players didn't take it seriously because it was a new innovation concocted by the French. It was only a 'tin pot competition' to them.

Some players got into trouble over alleged indiscretions on the tour earlier in the year. They were blacklisted by the Rugby Football League according to reports at the time. Many of the other Great Britain squad members boycotted the World Cup to protest their colleagues' treatment, including previous skipper Willie Horne. This is how Valentine got his chance to be captain.

Young Johnny Whiteley went on tour as an understudy to skipper Valentine. Whiteley told me many years later about the hilarious early stages of Great Britain's World Cup.

As the tournament was hastily put together, things weren't organised. When we got to France, all the other teams were wearing their traditional attire. Australia, New Zealand and France wore blazers proudly. We didn't have any official uniforms at all, just a mixture of outfits. The media got stuck into us.

I remember getting on the team bus after a training session at Rochdale. Joe Egan, the hooker for Great Britain after the War, was our coach. We were told that we couldn't take Joe with us to France, as there were no funds. We couldn't afford him.

Upon arriving in Paris, we couldn't find the ground and we had nobody to speak French either. It was a disaster. We eventually found it but no one was there, we couldn't get in. So we had to climb over the gates. Of course, when we got inside, there weren't footballs either! I remember one of us stuffing a vest into a sock and using that as a football. That was our first training session, in an empty ground, passing a sock around, deep in France.

These struggles could have easily turned Britain's tour into a complete disaster. It was comical, yet it brought them closer together. Throwing a piece of clothing around in the dark didn't sound like training but it started their campaign on a lighter note. The serious stuff could wait.

By contrast, France had all the odds stacked in their favour. Their record at home was pleasingly strong; in 1953 alone they had recorded wins against Australia (twice), Great Britain and Wales. So, like a python, the French team was coiled up and ready to strike.

Mobile forwards and speedy backs

France's tough and feared forward pack, who would go on to dominate in the World Cup, initially signalled their intent during their 1951 tour of Australia.

They terrorised their much smaller back-line opponents through their kamikaze approach to tackling and hard running style. The monster back-row pairing of Élie Brousse and Edouard Ponsinet after France's re-entry into Test match football in 1947–48 paved the way for other generations to follow. No opposition players were spared or taken lightly. It was pure smash and bash, brutal, bruising forward play. Whereas other teams like Britain and New Zealand could call upon some tough forwards, the French pack took it upon themselves to create fresh nightmares for their opponents.

Australian fullback Clive Churchill could testify to the Frenchmen's ferocity. The Kangaroos skipper, rated by many observers as the best fullback the game has ever seen, wasn't afforded any special treatment by the French forwards. He simply became a more prized target. In his biography,

Churchill remembered one particular encounter involving Brousse and Ponsinet.

During a Test match on the 1951 tour, Churchill put in a huge tackle on one of the French players. Ponsinet and Brousse dropped what they were doing and spent their remaining energy planning to pulverise the Australian captain. They got their chance soon enough. France launched a kick for Churchill to run back. The little fullback – standing at just five foot seven and weighing little more than seventy kilograms – got hammered by both French forwards, who knocked 'The Little Master' momentarily unconscious. Incredibly, Churchill managed to play out the remainder of the game. The two Frenchmen acknowledged the much smaller player's efforts after the match, praising his bravery. They weren't sure how he managed to play on.

Brousse, at ninety-seven kilograms, six foot one, was one of the biggest men to play for France during his era. In his book, *Champagne Rugby*, French rugby league historian Henri Garcia describes him as probably the best second-row forward in the world at that time, with exceptional attack and defence skills, and the possession of agility and speed that belied his massive frame.

Ponsinet stood slightly smaller at five foot ten and ninety-three kilograms but was still a giant in his team. Nicknamed 'Ponpon', he was super quick (running 100 metres in 11.4 seconds). An opponent's best course of action was to stand clear when Ponsinet ran at full pace.

After Ponsinet and Brousse retired in 1953, leaving scores of Australian, British and New Zealand players high-fiving in relief, prop Jean Pambrun and second-rowers Jean Audoubert and Francois Rinaldi continued the French style of super-strong, intimidating and mobile forward play. They possessed great courage too: Pambrun played with broken fingers in the final but finished the match.

Along with their predatory roles, the French forwards also had great passing skills and would be regularly called upon to shape many attacking raids in conjunction with their back-line colleagues. It was these skills that were magnified in the World Cup final, as once the French sensed an opportunity in broken play, their whole forward pack sparked into attack mode. It was a breath-taking skillset in an era where there was a definite split between the duties of backs and forwards. The French teams of the 1950s were well ahead of their peers in this way.

The French also brought in former Test players Jean Duhau and Rene Duffort as their coaching team. Duffort toured in 1951 as a player and, as coach, brought great game awareness to the side. Duhau played rugby union for France and was a member of the first French rugby league team in 1934. Both had independent responsibilities for attack and defence.

Halfback Jean Dopp started a trend of one-armed passing – sort of a basketball pass with one hand – that enabled their speedy backs to get maximum time with the football. Dopp gave his team great impetus, however one player in particular was instrumental in getting France to achieve what they did.

The pudgy little fullback

At five foot seven and barely seventy kilograms, with a rotund belly and inevitable cigarette in hand, French fullback Robert Puig Aubert left a huge impression on rugby league in the late 1940s and early 1950s. It wasn't due to his smoking, diet or tiny frame – but his brilliant kicking skills. He was the face of French rugby league for over a decade, embodying the amazing skill, flair and great moments that the sport could offer spectators.

Puig Aubert (real name 'Robert Aubert Puig', but for a back to front printing of his name in a newspaper article, was known as 'Puig Aubert') had cast an indelible

Puig Aubert, France's little champion, on the attack on the 1954 World Cup.
Rugby League Journal

impression on the Australian and French public after his phenomenal points scoring efforts in the 1951 tour. The boy from Carcassonne scored 236 points (106 goals, drop goals and eight tries). He regularly kicked conversions and penalties from his own half and his long punt was unrivalled in the history of the game.

His amazing deeds attracted huge interest from Sydney's St George, the richest club in Australia. The club offered him a three-year contract worth eight million francs plus a house and return plane tickets for his wife and young daughter. After much deliberation he decided to decline, preferring his French lifestyle.

At the height of his fame, Puig Aubert, or 'Pipette' (on account of his fondness for cigarettes – 'little pipes'), and his kicking made national headlines.

He also endeared himself to the general public with his cavalier attitude to training, diet and health. He hated training, chain-smoked and refused to tackle, surmising that it was the job of the forwards to do so. Although his girth was widening by the time the World Cup rolled around, he still inspired magic, notably in the French defeat of the Kiwis in the first pool match.

Duhau and Duffort focused much of their attack on fullback Puig Aubert's brilliant kicking game, along with using quick and powerful players across the park.

His place-kicking style left crowds stunned and thrilled. The fullback would place the ball, turn and walk back, then without a care in the world, run up and kick. He was France's talisman, captain and kicker, all in one.

Yet not everyone was enthralled by the French fullback. Australian captain Churchill was unimpressed and couldn't understand the hype surrounding his counterpart. Their running battles during the tour of 1951 – when a cocky and brash Puig Aubert declared to an incredulous Sydney media 'I have found Churchill out' – were classic acts of gamesmanship. In his autobiography, Churchill says that he didn't rate Puig Aubert as a great fullback at all, preferring the talents of Englishman Martin Ryan, Kiwi Warwick Clarke and others over the Frenchman. He admits his opponent's kicking deserved exalted status, but feels he should only be remembered as a great kicker for goal or in general play, but nothing more.

In their three-year running battle, Puig Aubert would have the final say against Churchill during the World Cup. In a tight affair during their final pool match, the French captain kicked a vital three goals in his side's 15–5 defeat of Australia.

His lack of preparation made his feats even more remarkable. *The Sydney Morning Herald* gushed: 'He is an absolute marvel. He smokes like a chimney, quaffs everything he can and has an absolute horror of training!' It is easy to see why the French public took a liking to the little fullback. He did amazing things to get French rugby league off the canvas and into the hearts and minds of their fickle public.

Bread, wine and cigarettes

Australians have always led the way in their approach to sporting excellence. Even in the 1950s, their national rugby league team would adhere to key principles including a steadfast commitment to diet, nutrition and exercise. A big part of their training regime was based on the work of Professor Frank Cotton, the father of modern sports science in Australia, plus swimming coach and lecturer in human physiology, Forbes Carlile.

According to John Bloomfield's *Australia's Sporting Success: The Inside Story*, both men successful researched and tested athletes during this decade. They wanted to understand who and what made success at the top levels of international sport.

France took a different approach. The 1951 tour was almost as memorable for the Australian public's reaction to the relaxed habits of the touring French team as it was for the competition itself.

The Sydney press was so shocked at France's outrageous drinking, eating and smoking habits that they were sure *Les Tricolores* would be overrun. To be at the pinnacle of your sport, as were the Australians, you must have an excellent training and diet regime, the cornerstone of all successful teams. France was about to be taught a footballing lesson by mighty Australia.

The fact that France made it to the final lacking a 'proper' diet speaks volumes for their achievements and raises the question: what if they had eaten right and exercised well? How much better could they have been? Bread, wine and cigarettes seemed to work well enough.

The man behind MacPherson

James MacPherson is not the first name you would associate with rugby league. After all, he lived over 200 years before

Dally Messenger and the All Gold's started rugby league in 1908. The convicted Scottish outlaw, though, was instrumental in galvanising the Great Britain team during the World Cup.

That's because Valentine, inheriting a patched-up squad, used the story of MacPherson to bring together his team and get them motivated, unified and ready for battle.

MacPherson was an outlaw in the north-east of Scotland who led a band of robbers some 300 years ago. No one would arrest him because he was such a fine swordsman, but as he came into the town of Keith through a narrow street, a woman sitting at a window above threw down a thick heavy blanket that entangled him so he could not draw his sword. He was captured and sentenced to be hanged at the Cross of Banff on 16 November 1700.

MacPherson was a fine fiddler, and he composed this tune the night before he was hanged. He played it on the scaffold, and offered to give his fiddle to anyone who would play the tune at his wake. No one would, so he smashed the fiddle. Anyone who had accepted it would have shown themselves to be a relative or friend of his and so liable to arrest themselves. Here is Robert Burns' version of 'MacPherson's Lament':

Farewell ye dungeons dark and strong,
Farewell, farewell to thee
MacPherson's time will no' be long,

On yonder gallows tree
Sae rantin'ly, sae wantonly,

Sae dauntin'ly gaed he
He played a tune and danced it roon
Below the gallows tree

It was by a woman's treacherous hand
That I was condemned tae dee
Below a ledge at a window she stood
And a blanket, she threw o'er me

'Untie these bands from off my hands
And gi'e to me my sword
There's no' a man in all Scotland
But I'll brave him at a word

'There's some come here to see me hanged
And some to buy my fiddle
But before that I do part wi' her
I'll brake her thro' the middle'

He took the fiddle into both o' his hands
And he broke it over a stone
There's no' another hand shall play on thee
When I am dead and gone

The reprieve was comin' o'er the brig o' Banff
To let MacPherson free
But they pit the clock a quarter afore
And hanged him from the tree

As a proud Scot – one of only two selected in the entire squad – Valentine created a strong sense of pride in the

Great Britain jersey. According to halfback Gerry Helme and winger David Rose (a fellow Scot), before each game, Valentine would start off by singing this song. It became a tradition for the team throughout the tournament.

Tintin's strike

French winger Raymond Contrastin was about average in height and weight for the French team. At five foot nine and seventy-eight kilograms, he doesn't immediately invoke thoughts of a runaway freight train.

Yet this was exactly his game – he employed a devastating mixture of strength and power, all in a relatively small body.

Garcia describes him in *Champagne Rugby* as a 'muscular pocket-battleship. Brave and direct, he takes the shortest route to the line. Known as "Tintin", he won't show his face if the team loses'.

Contrastin's power game was in full force during the World Cup, and he scored in every match. He crossed once against Australia two days before the final, twice against Great Britain and another in their first match against the Kiwis. He was at his try-scoring peak. He finished his career as France's second highest try-scorer in Test matches with fourteen, only one behind his teammate Jacques Merquey.

During the final, with Britain leading early, France needed to strike back quickly before half-time. Puig Aubert managed a forty-five-metre penalty goal to open his team's scoring.

Soon afterwards, Great Britain centre Phil Jackson decided to race out of the line and charge quickly at French hooker Jean Audobert. But Audobert, at five foot ten and one of the oldest of their squad at thirty, managed to duck under the harassing tackle and shift it wide.

With quick passing between forwards and backs – carrying out the coach's strategy of running the ball and creating space – the ball was shifted to right-winger Raymond Contrastin. He still had ten metres to go and three British defenders to beat.

'Tintin' slammed on a left-foot step at full speed. Bracing himself for impact, he ploughed through the flailing attempted tackles of British fullback Jim Ledgard and winger Dave Rose. Paper might have been stronger. They had no chance of stopping the pocket-battleship. Contrastin crossed the try-line and managed to improve the position for Puig Aubert to convert and take the lead.

The mainly French crowd were out of their seats with excitement. Yet Great Britain's halfback had a step of his own in store for the home side.

Helme's famous fend

Gerry Helme was at the peak of his powers when called upon for the Rugby League World Cup.

He played in the Ashes series and New Zealand tour earlier that year and turned himself into Great Britain's first-choice halfback with some excellent attacking displays.

However, his greatest achievement prior to the tournament was his starring role in the Challenge Cup final replay for Warrington against Halifax in 1954, which was played in front of a then world-record crowd of 102,560.

Helme capped a magnificent display by scoring the match-winning try in an 8–4 victory.

He was the first man to win the prestigious Lance Todd trophy twice (awarded to the annual Challenge Cup final Man of the Match, the crowning achievement in British rugby league).

Only five foot five and sixty-nine kilograms, Helme was the smallest player in his side. But he made up for this lack of stature with his eye for a gap, acceleration and wonderful tenacity.

He also had to work with a new halves partner, untried rookie Gordon Brown, who at twenty-four was an exciting selection. Regular five-eighth and skipper Dickie Williams missed the tour. New combinations needed to be established quickly.

Browne proved to be an attacking sensation during the early World Cup matches, scoring tries in each game. Helme deserves credit in building Browne's confidence, using his experience playing eight Test matches since 1948.

So when the World Cup final was in the balance in the second half, with France leading 9–8 after Contrastin's try, Helme stood up and provided a magic moment.

After accepting a pass from British second-rower Don Robinson thirty metres out from the try-line, Helme was faced with a moving wall of French defenders. Anticipating he would pass to Jackson on his left, Merquey rushed up and tried to put a hit on the British centre. As he did so, Helme subtly changed the angle of his run, sensing an opening with Merquey out of the defensive line.

His French opposite Antoine Jiminez, a taller man at five foot eight and a half, grabbed Helme's shoulders, trying to wrap him up with the football. But Helme stuck out a powerful fend and knocked Jiminez off his feet. He ducked and shrugged his way past the French five-eighth. With only second-rower Armand Save to beat, the Great Britain halfback easily sliced his way past and crossed for a try. It was the moment that turned the match.

Helme's sense of timing, vision and quick thinking broke the resolute French defence. Ledgard easily converted to make it 13–9 in favour of Great Britain with time running out. But France wouldn't give up.

Cantoni strikes

Sidestepping in rugby league in the modern era is all the rage. All the youngsters want to be Brad Fittler, Benji Marshall or Roger Tuivasa-Sheck. Yet these three talented footballers can thank French centre Jacques Merquey for really bringing the sidestep to life on the world stage. Merquey combined well with winger Vincent Cantoni to give France a further chance.

Cantoni made his Test debut in 1948. He'd been part of the rise of rugby league in France and was playing his eleventh Test match. His brother Fernand continued the Cantoni family tradition of playing in French rugby league teams by touring Australia a year later.

It was to be Vincent's last match in French colours. He had time for one more act that will go down as the most unforgettable try of the first World Cup.

Immediately after Helme's try, France managed to get possession and moved up to halfway. Merquey received the football in good position and made his move.

He managed to step and evade three Great Britain players like it was a game of tag. Hooker Sam Smith was made to look punch drunk, as France's all-time leading try-scorer put on his dancing shoes.

Having attracted these defenders and sensing an overlap, Merquey turned to his right and hurled a javelin-style pass to Antoine Jiminez. The five-eighth found Cantoni who had forty metres to run. But he managed to charge downfield and evaded what seemed like the whole of Great Britain's left defence, crossing in the corner for a magnificent try. From Merquey's brilliant footwork, to Cantoni's excellent finishing, France announced their dangerous ability to attack from anywhere on the park.

Britain bites back

A captain's true test is to galvanise their team when the chips are down. So Valentine responded by mobilising his forward pack. Their mission – tackle hard and run constantly at the tired French forwards.

They started to overcome the French, slowly through quick plays of the ball, then through quick attacking raids between the forwards and backs.

Great Britain centre Phil Jackson told me his side felt that could disrupt the French through imposing themselves physically. 'We thought we could overcome the French if we made it a tough game, with plenty of aggression, that they wouldn't be able to cope.'

The Daily Express writer David Nichols, writing of Valentine's testimonial event years later, summed up Valentine's inspirational ability.

> Valentine gave this untried British side inspired
> leadership, and the whole magnificent victory was
> founded on inspired forward play. Every man did his
> stint, and then got the ball away for the backs to use
> their pace. It was as simple as that.

France couldn't get back into the game. Great Britain kept attacking, particularly using quick men Jackson and Helme to tire the French forwards through short running bursts. Finally, after great discipline by the British pack, Gordon Brown scored again and despite another Puig Aubert penalty, the French couldn't break the British defence. Great Britain held on to win the first World Cup tournament.

This was their finest hour

British radio and television commentator Eddie Waring was on hand to witness one of the finest moments in British rugby league history, marvelling at the sight of Valentine and Helme being carried off on the shoulders of their teammates. He felt that the achievement was made even more special considering the upheaval and distractions that went on before the Cup.

To borrow from Winston Churchill, it was certainly Great Britain's finest hour.

A positive future

Valentine and his team were hailed as sporting heroes. The shock of victory took a long time to wear off, particularly for the British press.

Harry Sunderland, former Kangaroos tour manager, had great praise for the British skipper and his ability throughout the whole tournament.

> Valentine showed his true worth in co-operating with team manager Gideon Shaw in the development of that greatest aid to success – team spirit. He inspired every member of the Great Britain party by his own example. First against the Australians at Lyon, then against France at Toulouse, then, at Bordeaux against the Kiwis, David led the way to success. And when it came to the final against France in the Parc des Princes in Paris, David led his side to such a great victory that it proved to be the crowning point of his career.

Jackson echoed this sentiment. 'He was a great captain and a very friendly sort of man. Apart from getting through to us motivation-wise, he was very popular and well-liked.'

The *Rugby League News* was full of positive comments about Barrière and what the event did for Test rugby league. It proved a grand success in every way, and the French Rugby League authorities were widely congratulated on their enterprise and foresight in staging the World Cup. The other nations then resolved to stage a Cup series wherever possible.

Although a French victory in the final would have been a fairy-tale to tell the grandkids, Great Britain's backs-to-the-wall victory, Australia's shock early exit and New Zealand's excellent prior form leading into the tournament combined to make the event a real triumph.

Clive Churchill, although his team missed out on the final – still the only time an Australian team has not made a World Cup final – wrote years later that he was very impressed by what the World Cup represented, how it was run and how important it could become.

Backing up this achievement, the Great Britain side confirmed their status as the number one team in world rugby league when they reclaimed the Ashes the following

Skipper Dave Valentine and scrum-half Gerry Helme are carried aloft by the victorious Great Britain team after their win in the 1954 World Cup Final at Parc des Princes, Paris. Rugby League Journal

year in the United Kingdom. France was invited back to Australia in 1955 and had another series victory, and drew a series against the Kiwis 1–1 the same year.

New Zealand had some difficult years following the World Cup, losing series against Australia, France and Great Britain. They suffered from a tiny player pool and some key retirements. Promisingly, they managed to rebuild and blood new players in time for the 1957 and 1960 tournaments.

Valentine didn't get to enjoy the post glory-glow for very long – successive injuries in 1955 meant he was forced to retire early. His knees had just held out long enough to lift a World Cup.

He died in 1976 aged only forty-nine after developing a brain tumour. His immense contribution to Scottish rugby league was recognised in later years – Scotland's national player of the year award is named after him.

The inaugural World Cup confirmed the great potential of the tournament and helped shape international competition through to the modern day. Haphazardly put together, hastily run, but rugby league's version of a World Cup had begun.

Scoreboard: **Great Britain 16** (Brown 2, Helme, Rose tries; Ledgard 2 goals) defeated **France 12** (Cantoni, Contrastin tries; Puig Aubert 3 goals). Crowd: 30,368.

Match 2, 1960

THE QUEEN'S NOT GOING TO SAVE YOU NOW

Great Britain v. Australia

Odsal Stadium, Bradford, England
8 October 1960
World Cup final

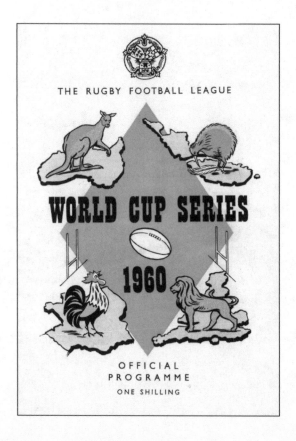

THE RUGBY FOOTBALL LEAGUE

WORLD CUP SERIES

1960

OFFICIAL
PROGRAMME
ONE SHILLING

GREAT BRITAIN	AUSTRALIA
1. Austin Rhodes	1. Keith Barnes (captain)
2. Billy Boston	2. Ronald Boden
3. Eric Ashton (captain)	3. Harry Wells
4. Alan Davies	4. Reg Gasnier
5. Mick Sullivan	5. Brian Carlson
6. Frank Myler	6. Tony Brown
7. Alex Murphy	7. Barry Muir
8. Jack Wilkinson	8. Dud Beattie
9. John Shaw	9. Noel Kelly
10. Brian McTigue	10. Gary Parcell
11. Derek Turner	11. Elton Rasmussen
12. Brian Shaw	12. Rex Mossop
13. Vince Karalius	13. Brian Hambly
Coach: Bill Fallowfield	Coach: Keith Barnes

Referee: Eddie Martung

On the face of it, Joseph Kittinger, the Soviet Union and the Australian rugby league team don't seem to share anything in common. But 1960 was all about gambling, a theme all three grasped. Kittinger recorded the highest ever altitude parachute jump, while the Soviets launched satellites into space containing dogs, rats, mice and plants. The Australian team selected a bunch of rookies for their World Cup campaign and put faith in potential rather than solid Test experience. Whereas Kittinger and the Soviets passed their challenges without issue, the Australians found it much more difficult. The team that had swept aside all nations in the 1957 World Cup hit a major obstacle on their way to the 1960 Cup: namely, an angry Great Britain team. It wasn't supposed to be like that. A new breed of rough-and-tumble Australians had given their fans a huge boost as they marked their fifty-year anniversary of being a Test nation with a decisive tournament victory. It was just what their local fans needed after an underwhelming World Cup three years earlier.

The Australians had quality and experience across the park. Players like Ken Kearney and Kel O'Shea were top-class forwards, while Brian Carlson's fullback play was as good as any on the international scene. Trouble struck early: they had three of their best players knocked out of the tournament with injury after the first match – regular fullback and captain Keith Barnes plus halves Keith Holman and Greg Hawick. It didn't matter. The rugby league world had better be on notice. Imagine what pain they could inflict with a full-strength team.

The memo didn't reach the British Isles, though. Sick of being smashed around like the little cousin in the 1957 series, a new breed of enthusiastic young players entered the Test ranks in 1958. Two players gave Great Britain the belief and courage to transform their side into world-beaters once again: a veteran and a rookie.

In the dressing rooms during the second Ashes Test in Brisbane, Great Britain skipper Alan Prescott's broken arm was dangling off his shoulder like a piece of thread. It was a gruesome sight, a memory that stuck in Eric Ashton's mind long after that moment. Indeed, the visitor dressing rooms at Brisbane's Lang Park looked like a war infirmary. As Prescott was getting bandaged up by team doctors, players were lying on the floor in agony: Eric Fraser had fractured an elbow, young gun Vince Karalius could hardly walk due to a bruised spine, Dave Bolton had a broken collarbone and Jim Challinor had smashed his shoulder.

Prescott decided to play the rest of the match. The courage and tenacity of the captain – along with a fired-up Karalius who moved into the key five-eighth role in Bolton's absence – inspired his team to a surprising, uplifting 25–18 win. British rugby league was back. Pride in the jersey – they got that back too.

Prescott was carried shoulder-high around the ground in Sydney after they won the third and deciding Test 40–17. It was his last act in a Great Britain jersey and he retired from all rugby league in 1960.

British team manager Tom Mitchell later spoke of his

'selfless sacrifice for his team and country, unequalled in any sport anywhere in the world'.

So when Ashton, who was elevated to national skipper in 1959, led his team out on Bradford's bleak Odsal Stadium in the World Cup final, he felt confident in his team's chances. The Aussies fielded a fairly young side – brought on by the double Ashes failures of the previous years – whereas Britain had a team of hard, experienced Test players. The rematch was on.

Another excuse for a punch-up

Rugby league players of this era believed they could get away with illegality and brutality on the field. Maybe it was because their matches weren't shown on television very often. Yet it was part of the game. Punching, kicking and stiff-arm tackles were standard fare. Players regularly carried on playing with broken limbs and bones, rejecting any medication to relieve the pain.

It was a real 'dog-eat-dog' world of rugby league, no favours given and none asked for. That was the game, particularly at Test level, where you needed any edge you could get to win.

The brawling nature of this era reached its peak during the 1960 World Cup tournament where players were sent off like drunken patrons thrown out of the local pub. During the Great Britain–France pool match, which Britain won 33–7, Karalius and French skipper Jean Barthe were both sent off for illegal indiscretions – the first time two players had been sent off in a World Cup match.

Referee Eduoard Martung tries to keep warring players apart in the Odsal Stadium mud during the 1960 World Cup decider between Great Britain and Australia. Billy Boston and Derek Turner lead the British charge against Australia's Gary Parcell and Brian Hambly. Rugby League Journal

In the final group match between France and New Zealand at Wigan, French second-rower Robert Eramouspe was sent off for reckless kicking. The Kiwis prevailed 9–0, their first win in a World Cup fixture. If the match had been played in a street, most of the two teams would have been jailed for assault.

Amid the thuggery that characterised this era, the British and Australian skippers could hardly be further removed from their brawling teammates.

Gentlemen captains

Eric Ashton and Keith Barnes were sensational players in their own right. They were also both great ambassadors for the game, respectful and very modest about their vast achievements. Yet it was their calm captaincy reigns for Great Britain and Australia respectively that confirmed their status as rugby league greats.

Both made their debuts in the 1957 World Cup, but in a quirk of fate, didn't play each other. With his long, lean frame, Ashton represented the newly fashionable archetypes of northern England at the time: tall, slim, polite and reserved.

Vice-captain Johnny Whiteley had only good things to say about his skipper and long-time teammate.

> Eric had this great charisma. He was very laid back; nothing fazed him. He was a good human being, very intelligent and a deeper thinker. He portrayed an inner depth about himself. Everyone worked for him. Just his presence alone brought the team together.

The centre carved out a stellar career at Wigan (eventually racking up almost 500 appearances) and was regarded as a deep thinker of the game. His regular wing partner for club and country, Billy Boston, was a major beneficiary of Ashton's talents (they scored over 700 tries together for Wigan alone). Ashton later coached Wigan and St Helens to Challenge Cup final victories and became the first rugby league player to be recognised in the Queen's honours with an MBE.

He saw his role in the three-quarters as creating space for others to score tries. Ashton was the master of delaying a final pass, as well as the 'scissors move' (where one player would draw opposition players and then give an inside pass to an unmarked teammate). He was all about precise timing, geometric artistry and physical power. During that World Cup, even though he wasn't the most experienced in the group, his players respected his cool head and intelligent view of the game.

Golden Boots

Players of the 1960s never got the chance to run around in bright red Adidas or fluorescent yellow Nike boots. Yet Keith Barnes still managed to get the nickname 'Golden Boots' during his long and successful career.

Born in Port Talbot, Wales, he moved to Australia at twelve and got into rugby league quickly, rising through the ranks, and played in the New South Wales club competition by the age of twenty-one. This is where appreciative Balmain fans gave him the moniker because of his supreme goal-kicking feats. He kicked 742 goals across his thirteen-year club career, including an amazing ninety in only his second season.

His outstanding accuracy across all conditions was sublime, remembering this was well before boot cushion technology and airy rubber footballs were introduced. We are talking about heavy leather balls.

Barnes performed his nerveless goal kicking for Australia, too, and after only a couple of years in the side became their number one goal-kicker and fullback (replacing Glyn Moses as fullback and Lewis Jones as goal-kicker). He was just the man to take over from the well-respected Dick Poole, who captained the 1957 World Cup team. Barnes ended up with fifty-nine goals in just seventeen Test matches.

During the second Test of the 1959 Ashes series, with Australia needing a win to keep the series alive, Barnes injured his thigh while kicking for goal and had to leave the field. His replacement, Brian Carlson, missed a crucial chance at goal later in the match. Australia lost by one point. If only Golden Boots had been there to take it, Australian fans lamented.

But Barnes wasn't named Australian captain just because of his kicking ability. He was as tough as any big forward, a trait you needed in generous supply if you had ambitions to play Test football in those days. Take his debut as an example – a 1957 World Cup match against New Zealand. Barnes fractured his cheekbone trying to tackle Kiwi prop Henry Maxwell head on. Instead of going off, he played the rest of the match and kicked five goals to guide his team to victory.

Putting blokes in hospital is what I do

Younger rugby league fans probably know him as the taller man embracing the shorter man featured on the bronze National Rugby League premiership trophy. Indeed, big Australian forward Norm Provan deserved to be immortalised after an astonishing career. He had great ball skills for such a large individual, but he is most fondly remembered for his great consistency and durability (he played at the top level for fourteen years from 1951 to 1965). At a hundred kilograms and 1.93 metres tall, he would be huge nowadays, but he was giant-like back then.

During his six-year Test career until the 1958 Ashes series, Provan had established a reputation as one of the greatest forwards in the world. No opponent fazed him.

So when Ashton turned around to see Provan on the turf in pain during this Test series, he was shocked. Gigantic British prop Brian McTigue casually walked passed the dazed Provan like an assassin who'd just completed his latest assignment. It was his work.

Ashton was stunned. Why did you do that Brian? Do what? Do that and put three other blokes in hospital? Just part of the game, he said. And he walked back to his mark without another word.

McTigue had honed his toughness and great strength in boxing. He'd had over thirty professional fights before taking up rugby league. Off the field he was shy, retiring and hardly said a word (what is it with all these legends of the game who have completely different personas off the field?).

Long-jawed lock Vince Karalius was also part of the British new brigade during that series. He had huge hands – the largest, Ashton said, he'd ever seen. The Sydney press had given him such endorsements as, 'he does everything to stir the blood of his opponents,' and, 'one of the most destructive players England has ever sent to Australia'.

Super fit and tall (five foot eleven), Karalius hadn't always been a human wrecking ball causing little Kangaroo backs to have nightmares. He needed a tough initiation to club football to transform himself to the cult figure revered in both Australia and Great Britain to this day.

After he got bashed around in his debut club match for Wigan, Karalius decided to analyse his game. By then he was a bright and up-and-coming young player, but he lacked the 'mongrel' that characterised his later legacy. After a chat with his father, who gave him some strong words of advice, from then on he decided he needed to be bigger and stronger than his opponents. Something had to change. He would no longer simply take lots of punishment. He would give it back 110 per cent. There would be a different Vince Karalius next time round.

He built his body though lifting weights and changed his attitude from a starry-eyed youngster to a no–nonsense wrecking machine that drove fear into hapless opposition players.

This stirring aggression caught the eye of the national selectors, who decided to throw Karalius into the most ferocious cauldron possible: an Ashes series in Australia.

After a solid display in the first Test win in Brisbane, the lock-forward decided to lift his defensive play to a new level in an effort to win the series.

'What he did that day [the second Ashes Test in 1958] was unbelievable,' said his teammate Alex Murphy. 'He wasn't going there just to tackle. The first thing he said was, "Let's put a move on." That was the sort of confidence he had.' Australian forwards in particular would feel his intensity and fierceness. Rex Mossop called Karalius 'the hardest of all the hard men' and wrote: 'For years he took my best shots without blinking. He demolished me on three separate occasions.'

Great Britain forward Geoff Gunney recalled that Karalius didn't just tackle his opponents, but picked them up and shook them as if he were a bear. He was a frightening prospect for even his own team, in an era in which everyone seemingly wore monster dress-up kits at Test level.

Despite his reputation, Karalius was never known as a dirty player. Murphy said that Karalius had a habit of bashing blokes around a bit on the footy field. But his efforts were just honest-to-goodness demolition jobs with every tackle, nothing illegal.

Rocky's star turn

Alongside McTigue and Karalius, second-rower Derek Turner completed the fearsome trio in Great Britain's back row.

Turner worked as a furniture removalist by day, lugging huge wardrobes and other large items around with his bare hands. Imagine the punishment he could dish out to an Australian, Frenchmen or Kiwi player? To him, they were just another item that needed removing.

He got his nickname 'Rocky' from world champion boxer Rocky Marciano whose tactic was to absorb every blow his opponent could dish out, before knocking him out.

Turner made a brief cameo in the 1963 film *This Sporting Life*, a story about a crude and violent Yorkshire coalminer called Frank Machin (played by Richard Harris), who is also a rugby league player. So the story goes, Turner's job was to punch Harris's character during a match. The director,

Lindsay Anderson, wanted it to look as real as possible – so 'Rocky' obliged by actually punching and knocking Harris out unconscious. Filming had to stop for a day to allow the actor to recover.

Colin Hutton, coach of the 1962 British team that toured Australia, thought there was never a harder man in rugby league than Turner, and he was as good as any lock-forward to have played the game. Hutton recalled a match for Hull FC 1957 when, nearing the end of his career, he played in the new position of second-rower (he was normally in the backs). He saw one of his teammates being manhandled by an opposition player in a large melee. Grabbing the first player he saw, Hutton found himself 'staring into the deep, dark eyes of Derek Turner. I broke out in a cold sweat and almost fainted'.

Television joins the big stage

Odsal Stadium could hold 100,000 people in 1960. But the Bradford faithful hardly filled the bleachers for the final – just 33,000 braved the elements that day. In editorials in the *Rugby League News* and official World Cup program, everyone agreed that the rise of television meant punters no longer needed to attend live matches.

Only 18,262 on average turned up to watch all the World Cup matches. Compare this with the Australian event three years prior, which managed almost double (35,000 over six games). The neutral matches didn't capture the British public's interest, and a crowd of 60,000 was needed for the two final matches to make a healthy profit. Only 3,000 turned up for France versus New Zealand.

The BBC unwittingly played a large part in the poor spectator turnout. Having pioneered live sports coverage in Britain with the 1956 Winter Olympics, they established the popular BBC *Grandstand* program two years later.

One Briton in particular was more enthusiastic than most about the rise of media coverage.

Eddie Waring wrote to the BBC asking for a chance to cover local matches as far back as the 1930s. After twenty years of nagging, he finally got his chance in the big time.

Waring could see the potential of televised sport long before it took off in Britain. After covering the 1946 Great Britain tour as a newspaper journalist, he met Hollywood star Bob Hope, who showed him through American football matches how successful sport on TV could be.

In the 1960s and 1970s, Waring rose to become the voice of British rugby league. Whether it was Tests, Challenge Cup finals or the local competitions, Waring was a fixture on the airways. He was the mainstay of winter in the north of England, with his unique commentary style that sounded like a cross between a Londoner who spoke 'the King's English' and a local knockabout lad from Leeds. In rugby league territories, he brought the game to life and became 'Uncle Eddie'.

Swapping the favourites tag

For all the Australians' huffing and puffing over their success, it was the British who were talked up by sections of the media. Waring felt their side touring Australia in 1957 would beat every team by at least ten points. After being hammered by the Aussies, who were playing at a level seemingly out of everyone's reach, the British selectors started to plot their revenge in time for the next World Cup.

Along with the gung-ho Karalius, a new halves pairing of Alex Murphy and Frank Myler was introduced to great effect. John Shaw took over the hooker's role and Brian McTigue joined in time for the 1958 Ashes series. Veteran wingers Mick Sullivan and Billy Boston formed a blockbusting attacking combination, with Ashton and Alan Davies organising things in the centres.

It was their no-nonsense forward pack of Turner, McTigue and Jack Wilkinson that helped instil confidence into a young team.

Johnny Whiteley (who didn't play in the final) was also confident about his side's chances leading into the tournament.

> We had a tremendous side. Most had been together from the 1957 World Cup, and again through the 1958 Ashes series. We had [Mick] Sullivan, [Eric] Ashton and [Alex] Murphy – it was a hell of a team with great camaraderie, who had to overcome lots of adversity.

Gasnier stamps his class

'He regularly made unwinnable games winnable.'

Norm Provan summed up Gasnier's brilliance perfectly. The final wasn't a great match by any means. It was a dull, thumping affair just like many others during the tournament. But for world Rugby League fans, it showcased the greatness of the greatest centre we have ever seen.

Gasnier's rise from St George's reserve grade side to the Kangaroos in the space of just two months in 1959 was incredible enough. But he offered the Australians a match-winning option on his own: he had style, pace and artistry. Watching Gasnier was like watching a thoroughbred streak his way to consecutive victories, with the other horses struggling to keep up. He was in colour while the rest were in black and white.

Only a year earlier, he had helped set up one of Test rugby league's greatest tries. After running seventy metres up-field, swerving through five or six players, he offloaded at the last moment to a willing teammate who scored. It was out of this world.

Back at Odsal Stadium, from the moment Ashton kicked off, Gasnier and his centre partner Harry Wells had giant targets on their backs. The British side knew that they needed to stop the two wizards out wide to stifle most of the Australians' attacking impetus.

Keith Barnes received the ball and gave it straight to Gasnier. The centre, with his high-knee running style, ran diagonally across the field and braced for contact with the rushing British defence. Just as Alan Davies went in with a swinging arm, the Australian ducked and sped away, going on to run fifty metres up-field. The play eventually broke down with Ronald Boden. In less than a minute, Gasnier had changed the game dynamic. That's as close as the visitors got to the try-line for much of the match.

The Times newspaper gushed afterwards:

Gasnier is already a legend at 21 and he contrived to
stamp his personality on Saturday's match … Now he
is ranked with, even above, the greatest ball carriers the
game has even known … If we remember anything from
this gloomy battle, it will be those few seconds of Gasnier,
a player the Australians already rate above the late Dally
Messenger, for long considered the greatest of them all.

Gasnier managed to create three try-scoring opportunities,
but they weren't capitalised on. The plays broke down after
each break. Perhaps the problem was that he had so much
ability and nobody else in his team was able to catch him as
he was creating opportunities. He was too good.

In 1962, at just twenty-two years of age, he was appointed
Australia's captain.

A broken leg in the first Test loss against Great Britain
in the Ashes tour of 1967–68 spelt disaster. Australia
retained the Ashes after a troubled tour, but Gasnier made
a premature return in a French provincial match at Avignon
on 21 December and again broke down, announcing his
retirement at just twenty-eight with a record thirty-six
Test matches against all nations. He went on to have a long
career as a league commentator with the ABC and died aged
seventy-five in 2014.

Parcell's mistimed punch

Late in the match, while Britain were holding out a
determined but increasingly frustrated Australian side, tensions
were threatening to explode. Referee Martung refused to

send anyone off despite repeated offside infringements and some illegal play. The match was seemingly beyond salvaging for Australia, but one incident in particular summed up the visitors' night.

Before the game, Great Britain singled out Gary Parcell as the Australian forward to target with some old fashioned off-the-ball niggle. He was central to the Australian 'engine-room'. Shut him down, the others will follow. Yet, unfortunately for Britain, Parcell took the punches and returned with even greater ferocity to the opposition.

This behaviour wasn't conclusive to winning a World Cup final, nor was it productive, but it might have given them some sort of physical edge. Break their legs and they are down some men, right? It was part of the game during this era.

In the haze of gloom, blood and white-line fever, Parcell was struggling in a ruck with Jack Wilkinson and a few other British players. The Australian decided to finish the contest then and there by throwing a punishing left hook. He connected. A player spluttered back from the impact in pain. The only problem was, it wasn't Wilkinson that felt the full brunt of Parcell's anger. It was his teammate Dud Beattie, who had come running in to help his friend.

When I spoke to Parcell, he was unflinchingly honest with his assessment of a fairly open era of rugby league. The first thing I noticed was how passionate he was about the game and how much he loved playing for his country. It was refreshing to hear his straight shooting, 'tell it as you remembered it' approach. He took me back to a time when 'you got fifteen quid for five months' work'. It was hard work, played by tough men.

He couldn't remember the Beattie punch specifically, but he told me the final was a tough match against a very good British side.

'It was just one of those things that happened back then. England were a pretty good side, it was a bloody hard game.'

He recalled an incident in an earlier Ashes series that illustrated the nature of the game back then, as well as why there was so much violence during that World Cup.

One of the funniest things happened in the previous year's Ashes series in England. Rocky Turner kept knocking Barry Muir over. So, Dud [Beattie] and I went to give him a stitch up and cut him across the eye. A fortnight later before the second Test match we were lining up for the anthems. I looked over at Turner.

I said to him, 'What happened Rocky, did you fall off a motorbike?'

Eric Ashton then piped up [At this point, Parcell changes his voice to a flawless upper-class English accent.]

'Steady lads, they're playing *God Save the Queen.*'

[Back to his Queensland drawl.] Beattie replied, 'The Queen's not going to save you now.'

Back at Odsal Stadium, Parcell kept taking punches, but his teammates couldn't seem to find a way through a punishing British defence. The rough tactics were working.

Murphy's big break

On the field he was known as yapper, a big talker, cocky and confident. He had amazing self-belief. Few would disagree that Alex Murphy is widely acknowledged as Great Britain's greatest halfback. Yet his Test career was almost ruined before he played a game.

On his first tour with Great Britain, the 1958 Ashes in Australia, Murphy was with Alan Prescott visiting a racecourse in Sydney, enjoying some Australian hospitality. Murphy was busy watching the races while Prescott was with a guest and Kangaroos halfback Keith Holman, who Prescott introduced to his companion as 'the best halfback in the world'. At this stage, Murphy didn't think he was going to get a game, being so young. So, overhearing this and without fear of retribution, told the entourage, 'That's a big statement considering he hasn't played against me yet'.

As luck would have it, Murphy was selected in the next Test match. As he ran onto the field, Holman yelled out, 'So, let's see what you're made of! Here we go!' The Australian walloped Murphy all around the park over the next eighty minutes. The Englishman later confided that he overstretched himself, instead of sticking to his strengths.

Tears streaming down his cheeks, the rookie halfback was so distraught over his performance that he ran up to his room at end of the match and bawled his eyes out. Luckily, skipper Prescott managed to convince team management that he was much better than he played that day – but only after giving the young player a grilling.

Murphy came back strongly for the second and third Tests, turning in a display that left many Australians gasping with amazement at the skills and pace of the young halfback. He was just eighteen when he made his debut, the youngest touring player for Britain at the time.

Murphy managed twenty-one tries in twenty matches on the Australasian tour, which also featured matches against New Zealand. With his team down to just ten men in the second Test against Australia, he helped steer them to a famous 25–18 win, scoring his first Test try. Murphy was also part of the even more famous 40–17 third Test routing of the Kangaroos at the SCG, with his second try.

During that final Test match, after two stellar performances, Holman sought him out at the end of the match and told him, 'You are the greatest player I've ever seen.'

Murphy combined blinding pace with extraordinary game sense, along with probably his greatest asset: genuine toughness. For one so young and so small in stature, his game-breaking abilities and defiance in the face of giant forwards created the profile for every five-eighth or halfback to follow. He was also a fantastic communicator on the field – leading to the nickname 'The Mouth'.

So when dark-haired Murphy grabbed the ball and tore down the right-hand side of Odsal during the final, neither the British nor the Australians would have been surprised. Dashing and weaving his way up-field, he created just enough time and space for Mick Sullivan to cross for the first try of the match. It was pure magic. Every Australian player's head dropped.

Australian halfback Barry Muir tried to put Murphy off his game by starting a fight with him. The kid from St Helens didn't back down, though. It was an ironic moment as in amongst all the physical battles and brawling on the field, both halfbacks played excellent games. Maybe they decided to fight to blend in.

Murphy went on to play twenty-seven Tests for Great Britain. The first rugby league footballer to have two testimonial matches, he became an inaugural inductee into the Rugby League Hall of Fame and was awarded the OBE for his services to the game.

Try-scorer Sullivan went on to become the most capped British player of all time (only recently passed by Adrian Morley), with forty-six Test and World Cup matches in a nine-year international career. His forty tries make him the country's leading try-scorer.

Australia had its own superstar trio of Gasnier, Raper and Provan, but they couldn't stop Murphy that day. His whippet-like run shook the match's previously dull contest wide open. Britain seized the initiative and never let go. There was more pain in store for the visitors.

Boston's third time lucky

When Eric Ashton was asked to choose his ultimate Great Britain team, he said he would have no hesitation in naming Billy Boston first, then fitting the other twelve players around him.

With such prolific talent as Johnny Whiteley, Alex Murphy

Sometimes it's the unconventional methods that work best on the brilliant. Billy Boston stops Reg Gasnier by employing a headlock. Rugby League Journal

and Ashton himself, how could he choose the stocky Wigan winger over everyone else?

During an interview in 2007 with the National Archive of Rugby League, Ashton remembered Boston:

> His ability was unbelievable. He ran fast enough not
> to be caught … They didn't get to him. He was an
> exceptionally good player, very versatile too. I remember
> one time [for Wigan] he moved into five-eighth and
> scored four tries. He had legs like sticks, but he could run.

Both teammates and rivals marvelled at his abilities. Australian great Johnny Raper noted that close to the line, he was unstoppable. According to teammate Karalius, Boston wasn't actually as big as people made him out to be, but he was very powerful and had a remarkable sidestep.

Boston also possessed great timing on defence too. As he became more experienced, he perfected a great ball-and-all-tackle, wrapping up the man and the football at the same time, that few managed to evade.

After missing the 1954 and half the 1957 event due to injury, Boston was looking forward to finally completing a World Cup when 1960 came around. Yet luck wasn't kind again. Boston tore his thigh muscle a week before the World Cup was due to begin. He couldn't believe it.

He managed the injury playing in a match against Whitehaven, then had to withdraw a few minutes into the first training session. His tournament chances were looking grim. But the Great Britain selectors invested great faith and extra time in Boston to ensure he would be fit to play the first World Cup held in England. It was a marquee event and they wanted one of their marquee players on deck.

Boston came through, just in time. Winger Jim Challinor was named to play the first two pool matches, as Boston was still recovering. But the big Wigan player reclaimed his spot for the final.

At last, Boston's moment arrived. After six years and three World Cups, this was Boston's final shot at glory. Australia chose the eighty-eight-kilogram (fourteen-stone) Brian Carlson to mark him.

It didn't work. The British winger managed two line breaks in the first half alone and easily overshadowed his opposite number. His hulking, bustling runs haunted Australia's edge defence, and he managed some punishing tackling of his own too.

The final continued, without much real football being played. Neither side could get momentum and both defences held firm. Britain had the bulk of the territory and possession, but the Australians refused to yield. It was slogging, sloppy and gut-busting, the sort of match that wouldn't make the weekly TV highlights today. Like many big football matches, the result came down to whose nerve would break first, or which individual would make that telling contribution.

With only an Austin Rhodes penalty goal to show for their dominance, Great Britain led 3–0 with ten minutes to go. They managed surge after surge into the Australians' half. With the game still in the balance at 3–0, Boston received a pass via Karalius and Ashton with an outside man to beat. He put on a huge left sidestep, brushed past a defender and raced away to score the first try of the match. Rhodes converted from the side-line, increasing the score to a 7–0 lead. Finally, Boston could call it 'third time lucky'.

Can you please speak English?

Whatever the personal animosity between Britain and Australia during that World Cup series, the rising frustrations that reached a crescendo in the final were also due to the referees' inconsistent displays. Referees Eric Clay and Eddie Martung were not far from controversy throughout the tournament.

Clay had only refereed one series (the Ashes of 1959/60) before being appointed to partner Martung for the 1960 World Cup. He went on to referee another Ashes series in 1963/64 and two series between Great Britain and New Zealand.

Test players interviewed for this chapter had differing views on his performance but in later years he became the first celebrity referee during his appearances on the BBC's *Grandstand*. He undoubtedly did lots to lift the profile and awareness of rugby league referees during his long career, regardless of any criticism that went his way. His most controversial moment came two years later during the third 1963 Ashes series Test.

Nicknamed 'Sergeant Major', due to his firm and heavy-handed refereeing style, he sent three players off in one of the most brutal Test matches ever played. Barry Muir, one of the Australians sent off, approached Clay after the game and told him, 'You robbed us.' Clay reportedly responded, 'Barry, I've got to live here.'

Clay died in 2007, aged eighty-five, after a short illness. Sports journalist Dave Hadfield wrote in *The Independent* newspaper, 'Even though he had retired from refereeing for 35 years by the time of his death, "Sergeant Major" Eric Clay remained the most memorable and instantly recognisable figure ever to officiate at rugby league matches in Britain'.

Frenchman, Martung had played as a junior when rugby league was introduced in France in 1934. By 1960, his day job was Chief Inspector of the Bordeaux Police Department.

Coming into the tournament he'd only refereed Tests with France (against Wales, England and Australia), and his English was said to be very limited. This was a huge problem when it came to the matches which exclusively featured New Zealand, Australia and Great Britain.

In a controversial decision, Martung got the nod to referee the World Cup final. Unfortunately, his performance warranted close scrutiny afterwards. *The Sydney Morning Herald* lambasted the referee the next morning, lamenting that his inept display cost both sides a decent match.

Martung's major problem was his failure to take action during the match. Despite the numerous illegal activities by both teams, Martung's sternest action was to caution Turner and Parcell early in the first half and his refusal to send anyone off. It was at this point that the British pack pounced, deciding they could get away with anything and not be penalised for it. According to the *Herald*, they remained offside for the whole match, with the margin increasing the longer the game went on. The match continued to be a drab mixture of collapsing scrums and close-quarter football, with only Gasnier and Murphy lighting up the dark Bradford pitch.

Last chance saloon for the Aussies

Boston had Carlson's measure for most of the match. Yet the Australian kept pressing forward, trying things, being positive. No Kangaroo side backs down; it is in their psyche to battle until the final whistle.

So when Australian five-eighth Tony Brown managed a brilliant diagonal run across the field after ducking three attempted tackles, Carlson was lurking in support. He caught an inside ball and streaked away for a try, the first points for Australia.

Brown was one of the few players who survived the mass changes rung by the Australian selectors after the 1958 and 1959 Ashes series, helping his team to tight wins against France and New Zealand during the pool matches. The final turned out to be his last Test for Australia. Had he done enough?

The Australians kept up the attack. Second-rower Elton Rasmussen dramatically increased the anxiety levels of most in the crowd when he found a gap in the British defence. It was a case of shimmy, shimmy, bang and Rasmussen was away down the field, with four British defenders grasping at thin air in his wake. Halfback Barry Muir ran up with him on the inside, but Boston wrapped up the halfback with one of his patented bear tackles. It was a crucial tackle and stopped Australia in their tracks.

With one more scrum for the British, time was running out. Waring, commentating at the time, thought there was another two minutes to go by his watch. But Martung suddenly blew his whistle. Just like that, the match was over.

Murphy hoofed the ball high into the air in celebration. His teammates raised their arms in a mixture of relief, exhaustion and delight. Great Britain was a World Cup champion yet again.

They should still be celebrating

With champion players like Karalius, McTigue, Sullivan and Murphy, the victorious British side were on the cusp of a prolonged spell of domination. Yet Australia and New Zealand ensured that the next few years would be hard-fought ones for Great Britain.

Britain managed a closely fought Ashes series win in 1962. But Australia proceeded to win the next three, home and away, until the 1970 World Cup rolled around. There was talk of asking South Africa to join the world tournament potentially in the early part of the decade, but their game wasn't deemed strong enough.

The French continued to fight hard, losing close series against the Australians in 1963, 1964 and 1967/68, before reaching the final of the World Cup in 1968.

Finally, after years of being on the wrong end of some big scorelines, the Kiwis had a breakthrough period of success. No other side got close to the New Zealanders in the first part of the 1960s. In the period 1960–64, they were unofficial world champions, achieving the best record of any international team.

Their inspirational back-row trio of Mel Cooke, Don Hammond and Ron Ackland led their team's defence superbly, along with prop forwards Maunga Emery (grandfather of modern-day great Stacey Jones), Sam Edwards and hooker Jock Butterfield, who formed a tough and daunting front row. They also unearthed a wonderful talent called Roger Bailey, a try-scoring phenomenon who, according to New Zealand Rugby League historians John Coffey and Bernie Wood, was a hugely gifted attacking player.

After three World Cups in seven years, the Rugby League Federation decided to shelve the tournament for a while. France had a dip in competitiveness and wasn't deemed ready to play in a 1964 event, so for eight years the international landscape consisted of Ashes and Test series for all four major nations.

Ten years after Britain's triumph over Australia in the 1960 final, the two teams would play probably the most talked-about match in rugby league history.

Scoreboard: **Great Britain 10** (Billy Boston, Mick Sullivan tries; Austin Rhodes 2 goals) defeated **Australia 3** (Brian Carlson try). Crowd: 32,773.

Match 3, 1970

WIN THE FIGHT
TO WIN THE GAME

Great Britain v. Australia

Headingley, Leeds, England
7 November 1970
World Cup final

GREAT BRITAIN	AUSTRALIA
1. Ray Dutton	1. Eric Simms
2. Alan Smith	2. Mark Harris
3. Frank Myler (captain)	3. John Cootes
4. Syd Hynes	4. Paul Sait
5. John Atkinson	5. Lionel Williamson
6. Mick Shoebottom	6. Bob Fulton
7. Keith Hepworth	7. Billy Smith
8. Dennis Hartley	8. John O'Neill
9. Tony Fisher	9. Ron Turner
10. Cliff Watson	10. Robert O'Reilly
11. Jimmy Thompson	11. Bob McCarthy
12. Doug Laughton	12. Ron Costello
13. Malcolm Reilly	13. Ron Coote (captain)
14. Chris Hesketh	14. Ray Branighan
15. Bob Haigh	15. Elwyn Walters
Coach: John Whiteley	Coach: Harry Bath

Referee: Fred Lindop

Harry Bath, the master coach, threw up his hands in exasperation. His first stint in charge of the Australian team in the winter of 1962 couldn't have gone worse. Not only did his team suffer a humiliating 1–2 series loss to Great Britain – some fans were still trying to get over the 1960 World Cup final loss inflicted by the Lions – but worst of all, his players didn't seem to care.

Bath was one of the great players of his generation, but he never played for his native Australia. He decided to play much of his career in England along with try-scoring superstar Brian Bevan. In his early career he was selected to play for Australia on a couple of occasions, but serious injury prevented him from taking the field. It was a quirk of his footballing story.

When he returned to his homeland, the second-row forward produced a stellar couple of seasons for St George, including a record-setting year in 1958 (a club record of 225 points that is likely never to be beaten). Yet at thirty-four, in 1959, he called time on his playing career.

Bath decided to take up coaching shortly after retiring, and in 1961, joined the New South Wales coaching panel. It was his deep understanding of the British game that excited the Australian Rugby League; such knowledge would be invaluable when used against the touring Great Britain team of 1962. So, Bath was appointed sole selector and coach to try and claim the Ashes once again.

Eric Ashton's experienced British team tore the Australians up in the first Test at the Sydney Cricket Ground. Mick Sullivan and Ashton scored braces while

Billy Boston, Dick Huddart and Derek Turner also crossed. The end result of 31–12 was a disaster. It didn't get any better in the second Test. Boston grabbed a double this time as the visitors managed a 17–10 win. By the final match, Bath was at the end of his tether. The Australians managed an 18–17 victory at Sydney, by virtue of scoring four tries to Britain's three.

In Bath's first series as coach, he decided to trust his team to look after themselves off the park. They were grown men representing their country after all. His leniency backfired spectacularly. The 1962 team abused their coach's gesture of good faith by trashing hotel rooms and misbehaving. They certainly didn't seem to take their responsibility of being professional footballers seriously.

Disillusioned, Bath stepped down as national coach. He moved into hospitality, along with club coaching gigs and driving a taxi. The Australian job was off the radar. Between 1963 and 1967, Arthur Summons, Reg Gasnier and Ian Walsh all had turns as the Australian head coach, but none lasted more than a couple of years at a time. Bath might have moved on from the idea, but Bill Buckley, Australian Rugby League president, was convinced that he should have another go. It had to be the right time, the right assignment. Things within the coaching set-up needed to change; the coach and management needed to be able to control their players and get respect. So, in what may or may not have been a chance encounter, Bath picked up Buckley in his taxi one day. It was during this trip that the passenger asked his driver whether he would consider coaching Australia again.

Buckley insisted things would change, and that Bath would have the power to discipline his players. That was priority number one. The small matter of a home World Cup was another huge incentive. Thirdly, he would be in the rare position of coaching both a club (Newtown) and the national side. So, still wary, Bath accepted his old job back as Australia's coach.

Clancy Kingston joined his management team. Kingston's responsibility as team manager was to help keep discipline within the playing group. With the start of the 1968 World Cup fast approaching (which Australia went on to win undefeated), he and Bath devised a simple way of ensuring his players would behave: for any damage to property or accommodation, they would simply take the money straight out of the guilty players' pockets. It worked.

On the park, Bath's Australians had a side laden with great talent, like Bob Fulton, Graeme Langlands, Arthur Beetson, Billy Smith and Johnny Raper as skipper. With his players in check and success on the field, Bath, the 'Old Fox', decided to extend his stay as head coach.

Ken Arthurson was appointed team manager for the 1970 World Cup. It wasn't a great fit to start with as the two men clashed regularly. Arthurson, according to Bath, wanted to coach and pick the team as well as carry out his manager duties. So, Bath decided to watch Arthurson 'stuff it up', which came true. Australia lost to both France and Great Britain, the former being a big surprise. Bath had had enough and took the coaching reins back in time for the final.

Bath liked discipline and order. It didn't always rub his players up the right way, but over time, there was a real respect for his determination and efforts as the Australian coach.

Winger Lionel Williamson, who was selected in both his 1968 and 1970 World Cup teams, was a big fan of Bath's coaching style.

> He was a very good coach. He'd played in England, so
> knew their patterns. He could find a hole in a brick wall
> [talking about attack] and had a great ability to coach
> the game. He got the best out of his players; he was very
> easy to talk to. I had no issues with his style at all.

Bath set harsh fitness regimes throughout the tournament that changed every few days. One example was reported by an English journalist, who noted he made his players train in gale force winds in a hailstorm at Huddersfield. At the end of each day, at 5pm, he would go through tactics and strategies in order to win the Cup.

As a way of getting inside knowledge of the British game, Bath brought a former British club forward to training during the tournament. As the Australian team were working on scrums, the first wisdom the forward passed on was to grab your opposing prop's roll of belly fat. In British club rugby league terminology, it was called 'nipping', and was used to put opponents off. It was a masterstroke and worked sensationally during game day. The World Cup final beckoned.

Setting the scene

Australian prop Jim Morgan and British counterpart Cliff Watson were close friends, who had grown up in very different surroundings: Morgan in the rural New South Wales town of Maitland, Watson in the outer London borough of Stepney. They were hard men in an era of even tougher football. Watson was an experienced Test player when he faced off against the comparative rookie Morgan in the 1970 Ashes series. Yet it was during that series that the two combined to create a moment that defined a generation of Anglo-Australian sporting contests, particularly in rugby league terms.

The Kangaroos, coached by Arthur Summons, were hammering the visiting Great Britain side in the first Test. Tempers were rising and the British forwards were not enjoying it as much as their opposition. These frustrations came to a head when, after some stern, up-and-close words between the two, Morgan started a head-butting duel with Watson, provoking what was later to be called one of the most infamous, crazy incidents you will ever see in sport.

Watson recalls that moment well.

> He [Morgan] tried to put a hit on me [with his head into my face], so I thought I'd turn around and show him how it was done correctly. I did. Consequently he's had a funny nose. Since then we've been very, very good friends.

It's funny how players can be violent towards each other on a football field, but as soon as the final whistle sounds, become close mates. Throughout every World Cup, many players have recounted similar stories.

Depending on who you believe, Watson was credited as bringing what's known as 'The Liverpool Kiss' to Australia. Head-butting as a form of fighting may have originated in the docks of Glasgow or Liverpool's mean streets, but to a generation of Australian rugby league fans, the term was brought into their vernacular in Brisbane that Saturday, 6 June 1970. Some speculated that the two props were just celebrating their tries: Watson scored one, while Morgan got two (the latter's only tries in Test football). Whatever the motivation, both players would be reminded of that incident for years to come.

Back on the pitch, although the British players looked like they lacked fitness during that series, they still managed a surging 2–1 win with some outstanding individual efforts from tough prop Malcolm Reilly and exciting halfback Roger Millward, who had made a big impact on the preceding Ashes series.

Rulings and sponsorship debacles

Top-level rugby league matches today can be very formulaic. Get to your six tackles, kick, defend and repeat. Yet in the 1950s and 1960s, games were free-flowing affairs, complete with sweeping back-line movements.

Prior to the late 1960s, there were no limits on how many tackles teams could take before they needed to hand over possession. One club match in England forced a radical change, though. Huddersfield, playing against Hull in 1966, kicked off and only touched the ball twice in an entire half. It was farcical. Luckily, the sport's administrators took action, quickly, and Britain's rugby league power brokers proposed a new four-tackle limit ruling soon after this match. The Australians agreed to it too. In 1967, the rule was adopted: teams now had a maximum of four tackles to use the football, after which time there would be a change of possession.

As the game was getting used to this innovation, administrators were also dealing with a major problem off the pitch.

Once the 1970 World Cup rolled around, the issue of sponsorship came into focus.

The British Rugby Football League administrators ruled that the magnificent trophy donated by Paul Barrière and the French Rugby League was to be replaced with a tiny, ugly cup. There was immediate outrage from both Australian and British sports media and fans.

Former Kangaroo Bernie Purcell penned his frustrations in a column in Sydney's *The Daily Mirror*. He was disgusted with the British Rugby Football League administrators, who'd decided to change the trophy, the format and even the name of the event without bothering to consult anyone. Instead of the World Cup series, the tournament was to be called the more American-sounding 'World Championship'. From the cup to the name, the whole saga was disrespectful, not just to the players who were slogging their hearts out during the event but to Barrière, whose legacy was forgotten thanks to some boardroom antics and a stroke of a pen.

Ironically, the company that sponsored the World Championship and donated the new trophy went out of business soon afterwards.

Coupled with the explosive battles on the pitch leading up to the World Cup, these off-pitch machinations meant that tensions were fizzing between the two nation's governing bodies.

During the course of the series, the original Barrière-donated World Cup trophy was stolen from the Australian team's hotel and was not recovered until twenty-five years later, when someone found it in a Bradford rubbish tip. It was returned to the Great Britain rugby league headquarters on 1 June 1990.

Counting the cost of a bloody Ashes campaign

The previously much-fancied Australians had big injury concerns leading up to the World Cup as they suffered the consequences of the brutal Ashes series earlier in the year. Both first-choice captains, Graeme Langlands (broken bone in his left hand) and John Sattler (broken jaw) were unavailable. Players who hadn't played well in the preceding Ashes series were dropped – the likes of Jim Morgan, Arthur Beetson and Phil Hawthorne.

The well-respected Ron Coote was named as captain, with experienced halfback Billy Smith as vice-captain.

Ken Arthurson had said before the tournament that he didn't think his side had a great chance of retaining back-to-back World Cups. He did, however, express great faith in what his players could do, effectively backing them quietly but giving them underdog status.

Of the team that had contested the 1968 final, Eric Simms, remained at fullback, Lionel Williamson on the right wing, Fulton and Smith kept their spots in the halves, and Coote took over Johnny Raper's lock position. The rest of the side were raw, but tough and talented.

Great Britain's team was hardly recognisable from the 1968 squad – only Cliff Watson, Mick Shoebottom and John Atkinson remained. Britain had to rebuild too.

Every team's chance at glory

Since 1954, there have been fourteen World Cup tournaments. The 1970 event has the distinction of being the most closely contested of them all. Each team scored well, but Britain had by far the best defensive play, and averaged just seven points per match scored against them.

In an exciting tournament that lasted less than two weeks, all four teams had a chance to make the final, going into the last round of pool matches. Great Britain won all their games, including an 11–4 defeat of the Australians, so were guaranteed one berth. The Kiwis, France and Australian all won a match each, but it was the New Zealanders' huge 11–47 loss to the Kangaroos that put them out of contention. That was the only blowout in a tightly contested event.

The exciting French side narrowly lost to the Kiwis (15–16) and almost overhauled the red-hot British, losing 0–6. France's brilliant winger Serge Marsolan scored the best try of the World Cup, a spectacular length-of-the-field effort against the Kiwis. But it was France's match against Australia at Odsal, the scene of the 1960 World Cup final, that was by far the most enthralling of the tournament.

Bob Fulton, playing at centre that day and later crowned Player of the Tournament, scored a try within seconds of the kick-off – probably the fastest in Test history. France managed to recover and stay in the contest, hitting back with some sparkling tries. Dramatically, with ten minutes to go and the scores level at 15–15, the French stole the game when five-eighth Jean Capdouze banged over a huge drop goal. The gallant French team had a major scalp and injected hope back into their campaign, winning 17–15.

Gibson's fitness revolution

Jack Gibson never coached Australia, but he set the foundations of their international dominance through his involvement at club level. He was a huge fan of American football and enjoyed their coaches' strategies, tactics and philosophies. He and fellow coach Terry Fearnley visited the American gridiron scene in 1972, and took this knowledge back to the Sydney club premiership.

No fan of motivational speeches, he instead instilled confidence in his players; 'preparation is everything' was his mantra.

The Australians embraced this new, professional era in the 1970s better than anyone, according to Fulton. Training and fitness became part of the professional footballer's make-up, particularly in club football. Gibson led the way with his teams, whose players were able to outlast all the others, thanks to their dedication to training, exercise and self-belief.

Fulton believes that the Australians shot ahead of Great Britain during the 1970s on fitness alone. Years later, the British were still trying to catch up. Bath kept to a strict fitness plan with his World Cup team, ensuring Gibson's legacy didn't go to waste at the international level.

During the week of the World Cup final, Bath drove his team even harder during training, mercilessly whipping them up into prime fitness shape ahead of the biggest match of the tournament. No wonder Australia was able to get through what was to follow: the most brutal, violent, infamous Test match of all time.

Bash, crash and roll

Great Britain signalled their tactics early in the match. They were frustrated. Violence, punching and off-the-play thuggery characterised their game, rather than set plays or tactical kicking plans. Lionel Williamson remembered, 'They wanted to bash and beat us. Kneeing, biting, gouging … It was really tough.'

Given the talent in Great Britain's team, it remains a great mystery that the team didn't play to their strengths and simply attack with the football. Their forwards were the envy of all the nations, with a talented back-line and the experienced Frank Myler as skipper, who was playing in his third World Cup. They also had the advantage of playing at home.

Prior to the match, the British side didn't seem to be very interested in playing a final, as they had easily won all their pool matches and wanted to simply get gifted the trophy for best points differential. But the World Cup organisers hastily arranged a final, much to Britain's chagrin but Australia's delight. There was lots of confusion and mixed messages.

The match eventually got underway. Britain had a lot of the possession in the early exchanges, dominating territory and field position, with Australia having to spend most of this early period in their own half. The visitors continued to defend stoutly in the face of some ferocious British play. Both teams got some early points – a penalty for Australia, a drop goal for Great Britain to level at 2–2 – but the hosts continued to try and bash the visitors off the ball. The photos from that time don't do justice to the brutal nature of play.

The footballing priest

Australian centre John Cootes was the only man who didn't throw a punch, kick or knee that day. A living footballing trivia question – the only Roman Catholic priest to play rugby league for Australia – he had moved to Italy to follow his calling and studied theology at Rome's Propaganda College. During his stay, he played Italian club rugby.

He decided to return to Australia after he completed his studies. Coached as a boy by Clive Churchill, Cootes was a good goal-kicker and a clever, attacking centre. He knew that when the punches started flying, he couldn't retaliate because of his faith and the strict code of anti-violence that accompanied it. His involvement was a remarkable sub-story during arguably the most violent period in Test rugby league history.

Cootes counts his lucky stars to this day.

> Luckily I was treated [by opposition sides] with great deference. They realised the restrictions I was playing under. If I'd lost my temper on the field, or been involved in some of the punch-ups, that would have been my last game of football.

British firebrand prop Cliff Watson tested this theory during a Test match. Luckily for Cootes, his players had his back.

> Cliff Watson thumped me one time. Billy Smith came over to me and said, 'Who was that who got you, Father?' And I said, 'I think it was Cliff Watson, Bill.' 'Don't worry, she'll be right.' Next time Cliff got the ball, he disappeared under a swarm of Australians.

Cootes waited patiently for an opportunity to inject himself into the game.

Lurching forward with aggression

Tall, lumbering and domineering, Australian lock John O'Neill complemented his aggressive play with monster-like looks. He played the enforcer role with gusto throughout his career. Along with many other forwards during the tough old days of the 1960s and 1970s, he often pushed the boundaries of what was legal on the field. Appreciative teammates gave him the moniker 'Lurch', given his similarities to the shambling butler on *The Addams Family*. We aren't sure if O'Neill ever appreciated it.

In the pool-play match between Australia and Great Britain, O'Neill was cautioned four times by referee Fred Lindop for rough play. Britain's players didn't forget the punishment that he dished out that day, perhaps knowing there would be a chance of meeting soon enough.

As the final continued, the British forward pack seemed to focus their collective efforts not in working as a team to defend well, but to incapacitate and target O'Neill. How the Australian lock managed to play on remains a mystery to this day.

During the course of the match, they head-butted, bashed, stomped and kicked him, leaving him bloodied and broken. But O'Neill didn't strike back. He never lost his cool. Skipper Coote and coach Bath issued him strict instructions before the match not to retaliate. It must have felt like a kick to his pride, but managing to bury his usually aggressive nature was now vital to his team's performance. Britain was penalised; Australia reaped the rewards through more possession.

O'Neill's courage lifted many of his teammates. Lionel Williamson was in particular awe of his sheer bravery. He looked over at the beaten-up O'Neill during the match.

'I remember John O'Neill's shin cut open. He said, "I'll just keep my sock up and no one will notice."'

O'Neill's left ankle was almost stripped to the bone during the first few minutes of the game. He emerged from a scrum scraped and cut thanks to some stray boots. There were no replacements in those days; he had to stay on. You could clearly see his shinbone when he took off his sock after the match. He also needed stiches for a nasty eye gash. He should have been in a hospital bed.

Like his blood-stained socks, O'Neill soaked up the fury of a brutish and violent Great Britain team that day. Hurt, dented, but not defeated, O'Neill overcame their barrage, driven by a single thought: win at all costs.

Battle of the halves

Roger Millward's injury-enforced absence from Great Britain's World Cup squad left a massive hole in their ability to bring variety in attack. The exciting youngster from Castleford offered a range of dynamic skills – an eye for a gap, great vision and the ability to read the play. He was instinctive and trusted his ability. Going into the final, Bath was delighted that Millward wasn't lining up that day. Lions skipper Frank Myler quickly responded by giving his replacement, Mick Shoebottom, a huge endorsement, going so far as to suggest that 'Shoey' was the main reason why Great Britain were extremely confident going into the match.

Shoebottom had played at fullback or centre in previous tours and finally got the chance to play in the coveted five-eighth role alongside Keith Hepworth. His skipper also felt that the number six spot was Shoebottom's best and was going to give the Aussies a big shock. Like Millward, he was tenacious, skilful and extremely tough. He offered more of a power game and, like his opposite Billy Smith, was aggressive. He was a ready-made replacement.

Conversely, the Australian halves pairing of Bob Fulton and Billy Smith had more of a settled look. The wholehearted Smith had a toughness that belied his small frame, with teammates like John Sattler and Norm Provan in awe of his ability to match it physically with much bigger players. He was a relentless, tireless performer, which was gold on this day of uncompromising Test football.

Teammate Mark Harris remembers one moment in the final that showed the measure of the man. Making his Test debut, Harris, as his legs were tiring, walked over to Smith. On the ground seemingly checking his socks, Smith was actually inspecting a huge open wound on his leg that went all the way to the bone. Harris had to turn away in disgust at the grisly wound. Smith, nonplussed, simply took the 'she'll be right' approach, up he went, then got stuck into defending against a barrage of British forwards minutes later. This act of sheer courage inspired Harris, who continued to play on with a renewed sense of energy after witnessing his halfback's horrific injury.

The blond-haired Fulton could have easily lined up in the white of Great Britain that day. Born in Warrington, he moved with his parents to Australia when very young. He based his game on quick acceleration, physical strength and a dedication to fitness and training; it was no wonder that this cannon-like defence earned him the title Player of the Tournament.

Britain's fullback Ray Dutton had fielded a kick just outside his own goal-line when he came sprinting back up the field, weaving between the first waves of Australian defence. But Fulton, the master tackler with impeccable technique, lined up Dutton front on then lifted and drove him into the Headingly turf. It was out of the coaching manual. The immediate threat dismantled, Fulton got back into the defensive line, ready for the next tackle. His performance was rewarded with a Man of the Match in the final.

Williamson's World Cup magic

Complementing John Cootes's efficient finishing skills was winger Lionel Williamson. According to pundits who followed his career, Williamson improved as he got more experience, and by the late 1960s, he had the safest pair of hands around.

He made his Test debut in the home World Cup in 1968 and managed to gain selection again for the 1970 event (bizarrely not playing a Test in between events). Now working at a boys' school in Queensland, alongside his responsibilities as Boarding Supervisor, he'd in all likelihood be sharing some insight into scoring tries and catching footballs. When I spoke to him, he remembered just how much his side were outsiders going into the second tournament.

> Great Britain was the favourite. We were a new side, just starting off like New Zealand. This was a new team, a new era. When we left Australia, we were never expected to win. France beat us in pool play, which was a bit of a shock. We ended up meeting Great Britain in the final, and it was tough.

After Britain and Australia traded early points, the visitors got the ball in the home team's half at last. With British players spread wide, Fulton passed quickly out to Bob McCarthy, who shot an outrageous overhead pass to Williamson just as the British ran up quickly.

Williamson started heading right, then swerved left in-field, wrong-footing Shoebottom and Atkinson. The British players collided with one another. This caused two reactions: firstly, it allowed Williamson to run past and score a try, and secondly and more crucially, Shoebottom injured himself after bouncing off his teammate. Williamson remembers the lead-up to his try vividly, taking a strong view that the British focused too much on smashing players rather than proper tackling, which aided his passage to the try-line.

> Syd Hynes loved bashing blokes. I remember seeing him and then getting past Atkinson, from there it was all over. Hepworth got me but I was over the line. I think they were too focused on knocking blokes' heads off instead of tackling me. During the lead-up and after I scored my try, their players were still trying to knock my head off.

The try and conversion meant Australia led 8–4. It was now that skipper Ron Coote really took control of his team, ensuring they were focused on their game plan – stick to your job, keep in control, be efficient and tackle hard. Williamson has only praise for his captain that day.

He was a great bloke. He had great knowledge of the game and led by example. He brought us together as a team – was a great leader. He told us, 'Just do your job', it was as simple as that.

With fifteen minutes left, British winger John Atkinson put his team back in contention with a big play. After Great Britain won a scrum against the feed, Hepworth passed it across to Atkinson, who stepped through a couple of Australian defenders to score a vital try right in the corner. Britain regained a glimmer of hope and celebrated. They remained in contention with the score at 7–12, but needed luck and everything to go their way. They received neither.

John Atkinson dives over in the corner for Great Britain's only try in the 1970 World Cup Final at Headingley. Rugby League Journal

Fisher's big mistake

British fullback Ray Dutton was one of Great Britain's best that day. Although Fulton managed to halt one of his earlier kick returns, Dutton showcased his brilliant evasive skills in a superb run late in the match.

With just over ten minutes to go, Eric Simms unleashed a huge mid-field bomb, with Dutton fielding it beautifully right in front of his own posts. The fullback then made a charging, elusive run up-field, swooping left diagonally then immediately right moving in-field, evading a desperate attempt by substitute Ray Branighan. It was the run that could have changed the match for Great Britain, as he reached halfway without any issue and with a possible try just ahead.

It was the next moment that summed up Britain's dreadful day.

Hooker Tony Fisher had never lost a Test match playing for Great Britain until that day; he was part of a five-game winning streak, debuting in the 1970 Ashes series. He'd had a fairly good game until that point. As Dutton raced past his own thirty-metre line, Fisher undid all of his fullback's great work by punching and throwing O'Neill to the ground, who was so dazed at this point that he probably couldn't stand, let alone defend himself. Play continued and Dutton slowed down. Lindop called time off.

The referee asked to speak to O'Neill, who had blood trickling down beside his right eye, next to his long sideboards. Lindop then spoke to Fisher, along with Doug Laughton, who was deputising while Frank Myler was off the field, plus Australian skipper Coote.

I imagine he said something like, 'We have ten minutes to go boys, let's finish the match without further incident.' Yet he still refused to take any concrete action. Fisher wasn't banished and Australia was awarded an attacking scrum.

It was at this point that something snapped in every British player's head. They were transported to a cage-fighting match, subconsciously trading their rugby league gear for boxing gloves and kickboxing equipment. From now on, the game plan was to hurt as many Australians as possible until the final whistle sounded.

A few minutes after the resumption in play, Shoebottom threw out a swinging arm in an attempted tackle on Simms, who luckily fell and managed to evade it; Malcolm Reilly, after being tackled by Bob McCarthy, threw a punch at the Australian but missed. Finally, Billy Smith took exception to Keith Hepworth and launched a kick to his back. It was random thuggery. Lindop stopped play, had a good talking to both captains and the players involved, but did nothing.

Hynes and Smith go for a long walk

Great Britain now had no chance of winning the game. They were resigned to an empty and soulless defeat. With the game now in injury time and the minutes winding down, Hynes and Smith decided to start a fight as the ball went out of play. They could have easily been two drunken patrons outside the local pub, fighting on the street. The fracas featured a mixture of punching, kicking and head–butts. Lindop decided fifty illegal acts was enough for one game and with a wave of his hand ordered them off the field. It had taken more than eighty minutes of play, and a result beyond doubt for Lindop to take a stand against the violence. Both Hynes and Smith didn't return to the field.

It was absurd. After all the brutality and illegal acts that had happened during the game, maybe for Lindop it was a token gesture to remove a couple of the players from the field.

As if the game needed more headlines, both players decided to give some more ammunition to the shocked rugby league media for the next day's newspapers.

In the most surreal moment of the whole match, as both players were walking off, Hynes patted Smith on the head and put an arm around him as if to say, 'Good job lad, you've done well.' The moment they were ruled out of the game, the aggression, the punching, and the violence stopped for the pair.

Later, Lindop admitted it was a tough match to control, given the physical nature of the game. He was only in his third season as a senior official.

The match had a couple more moments in store. Britain decided to try and go for one last play.

Britain's scrum-win

After the tense atmosphere died down and the banished players left the field, Great Britain got possession from a scrum only ten metres out from Australia's try-line in what was to be the last play of the game. Shoebottom took the ball and ran quickly, urgently, with his last surge of energy.

He weaved across a couple of defenders and managed to offload to lock-forward Malcolm Reilly, who was looming in support perfectly. With the try-line only a couple of steps away, the big forward knocked-on and the Australians celebrated. Game over. Lindop blew his whistle.

The crowd changed from frantic anticipation to a stadium-wide boo that reverberated around the ground. This wasn't supposed to be the result. The unfancied Aussies had overcome a towering British side that were at home, confident and seemingly ready for one last match.

The match was over. But the violence hadn't ended yet. Australian skipper Ron Coote remembered a shocking moment that happened soon after the final whistle blew. Eric Simms went to shake John Atkinson's hand – and the British player punched Simms in the chest! Local police swarmed onto the pitch; it was bedlam in broad daylight. That was the final act in a blighted but unforgettable match.

We put in the rough stuff

Both the Australian and British media feasted on what was a shocking day in rugby league's colourful history. The violence made a mockery of the term 'sport' and didn't do anything for a World Cup series that had a new sponsor, a new outlook and a new vision.

Alan Clarkson, writing in *The Sydney Morning Herald*, held the British players responsible, labelling their play as more like street fighting than football. As the game slipped away from them in the second half, they did everything they could – illegally – to stop the Australians. But the men in green and gold simply didn't blink.

The British press took it upon itself to stamp out the violence for good. *The Mail* newspaper reported that it wasn't sport, it wasn't entertainment, and it wasn't interesting. *The Daily Express* cast the match even further into the gutter, claiming that rugby league's identity was now confined to the rubbish bin and the people that play it were no better than common thugs. The papers had a field day, their attitude partly explainable by their long-time support for rugby union, rather than its professional cousin.

Alf Drewry, the intuitive *Yorkshire Post* sports writer, was baffled by what happened right after the whistle sounded: 'Players with swollen faces and black eyes were exchanging quips and bottles of beer as readily as they had been trading punches only a few minutes earlier – yes, even into overtime at the final whistle.'

Great Britain's manager Jack Harding didn't bother to defend his players' actions after the match, admitting his squad deliberately put on 'the rough stuff' and went out to bash their opposition. Watson admitted many years later that the only way to beat the Australians was to fight back hard against them or else they would walk all over you.

Johnny Whiteley, Britain's coach and a wonderful former Test player, also admitted his team lost its temper and discipline in the last ten minutes, which ultimately cost them the World Cup. He felt niggling wasn't part of the game plan, nor was anything they had subscribed to previously. It was disappointing.

Ron Coote with the infamous 'egg-cup' World Cup trophy. This was the first and last time it was used. Rugby League Journal

Whiteley today remembers a tough match and acknowledges Australia as the rightful winner on the day. He doesn't subscribe to the theory that his side went in with a scripted plan to bash the opposition.

> We were favourites to win and had a great side. A lot of what happened in that last ten minutes was to do with frustration. We lost the fight, the battle, the match and ultimately the World Cup. It was a typical Ashes battle – hard fought and tough. The Australians deserved to win that match.

Winger John Atkinson went as far as making a public apology to Eric Raper years later for his actions at the end of the match. He said he wasn't sure what was going through his mind when he punched Simms and admitted the team felt jaded after a long season.

Britain were awarded nineteen penalties to Australia's seven, but they didn't make the most of those chances. This was probably one of the reasons why Coote was so proud of his team that day, being able to absorb pressure and execute their skills effectively.

He felt it was the toughest game he had ever played in; some of the brutality was just incredible. Australia wasn't expected to win and the British kept getting more hostile as the game kept slipping away. It was one of the proudest moments of his life.

Williamson was elated and felt it was the start of some great Australian teams to come. 'The win meant everything to us. It was very different to nowadays, no one was branded as a superstar. We just went back to club football. We knew this was a formation of a good young team.'

Team manager Ken Arthurson called Australia's win in the World Cup final 'one of Australian Rugby League's proudest days'. After the match he said to his players: 'I am proud of you – it was the most courageous performance I have ever seen on a football field.'

As Coote was awarded the World Cup trophy, he held it up with one hand, looking more like a patron in the local trivia night with a glass of beer. But that tiny trophy meant everything to an Australian team who showed their real class on a day on which the meaning of the sport was questioned and brought into disrepute.

Disgruntled British fans could be heard yelling, 'Go home you bums!' as the brave Australian skipper celebrated with his team on the pitch. It was certainly a peculiar end to an otherwise close and skilful World Cup tournament. But the question remained: could future World Cups survive another thuggish replay of that day in Headingley? What could the rugby league administrators and national bodies do to ensure that the brutality of the day would never be repeated? And could rugby league come back from it?

Ironically, the 1970s featured four World Cup tournaments, the most of any decade. The poor spectator numbers for the 1970 event – most matches featured less than 10,000 people through the turnstiles – did little to discourage rugby league governing bodies. Competitiveness was back, the product needed some tweaking, but there was an appetite for Test rugby league. The next event was held only two years later, with plans to extend beyond Britain.

Rugby league embraced a more professional era, with the Australians desperate to make up for their lack of success in the earlier World Cups. Britain needed some new heroes to get the public back on their side, France was able to still spring the odd upset, while New Zealand were competitive against Britain and France, but lost every match they played against Australia.

The stage was set for a galvanised Australian team to shine. They were ruthless, effective and dominated almost every series or tournament throughout the decade. Great Britain still had one trick up their sleeve; their fans only had to wait a couple of years to make up for the crushing 1970 World Cup loss in a display of football that still resonates today.

Scoreboard: **Australia 12** (John Cootes, Lionel Williamson tries; Eric Simms 2 goals, field goal) defeated **Great Britain 7** (John Atkinson try, Ray Dutton goal, Syd Hynes field goal). Crowd: 18,776.

Match 4, 1972

ONE LAST ROAR AFTER A DRAW

Australia v. Great Britain

Stade de Gerland, Lyon, France
11 November 1972
World Cup final

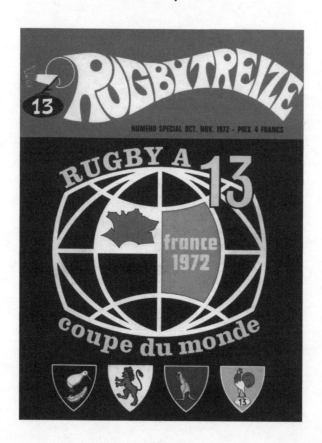

AUSTRALIA	GREAT BRITAIN
1. Graeme Langlands (captain)	1. Paul Charlton
2. Ray Branighan	2. Clive Sullivan (captain)
3. Geoff Starling	3. Chris Hesketh
4. Mark Harris	4. John Walsh
5. John Grant	5. John Atkinson
6. Bob Fulton	6. John Holmes
7. Dennis Ward	7. Steve Nash
8. John O'Neill	8. Terry Clawson
9. Elwyn Walters	9. Mike Stephenson
10. Robert O'Reilly	10. David Jeanes
11. Arthur Beetson	11. Phil Lowe
12. Gary Stevens	12. Brian Lockwood
13. Garry Sullivan	13. George Nicholls
Coach: Harry Bath	Coach: Jim Challinor

Referee: Georges Jameau

In November 1972, the world was still coming to terms with the horrors of Munich in September when a Palestinian extremist group killed eleven Israeli athletes competing in the Olympic Games. Terrorism had never been as public as it was that day. World leaders condemned those involved, and the rest of us still tried to get our heads around it. What was the world coming to? It was one of the most shocking events of the 1970s.

The ABC's Jim McKay, a sports broadcaster who assumed the duties of a news anchor as it unfolded on live TV, gave a solemn address after he learned the fate of the hostages: 'Our worst fears have been realised tonight. They have now said there were eleven hostages; two were killed in their rooms yesterday morning, nine were killed at the airport tonight. They're all gone.'

Less than two months later, the Great Britain and Australian rugby league teams did their best to give some joy back to their fans with a display that will go down as one of the most talked about Test matches in history. Luckily for the tiny crowd of less than 5,000 in the Stade de Gerland in Lyon, southern France, the World Cup final had a mixture of individual brilliance and great stamina by some sensational athletes.

The Lions and the Kangaroos had met many times over the previous couple of seasons, and the two captains who fronted up that clear afternoon were among the most inspiring to have ever worn their nation's colours. On the British side, Clive Sullivan, who refused to give up despite brutal physical and personal setbacks; and for Australia,

Graeme Langlands, the bold, brash and gifted fullback, whose athletic talent would not look out of place in the Olympics.

Britain surged into the final without any major problems, casting off Australia, France and New Zealand with consummate ease. In an era in which Test rugby league generally featured low-scoring, slogging contests, the Lions showcased their brand of skill and pace in the tournament.

Their back three of Paul Charlton, Sullivan and John Atkinson were excellent counter-attacking runners, with a powerful engine room of goal-kicker Terry Clawson, David Jeanes and the crafty Mike Stephenson at hooker. Jim Challinor was a steady influence as coach, respected by all, having appeared for Great Britain in the 1960 World Cup.

France to rise again

As Great Britain and Australia's skill level improved, the fortunes of the other two 'Big Four' nations – New Zealand and France – continued to wane. While the Kangaroos and the clubs in Australia invested heavily in training, preparation, strength and fitness, the French and the Kiwis were getting through the 1970s by cobbling teams together at the last minute, with the odd player defecting to the professional ranks in Australia or England.

Although France made the World Cup final in 1968, their battle to win the hearts and minds of their public and their government – the latter still intent on having rugby union as the country's 'real' form of rugby – wasn't going well. The French team's more than credible performances in the 1970 Cup helped their governing body mount another challenge to spread rugby league's brand in the south of the country.

French Federation president René Mauries had battled hard to keep the tournament in France. After all, the French administrators viewed it as a chance to continue to grow the game there. Hosting the World Cup with the sport's biggest names was a huge fillip and one Mauries and his colleagues desperately wanted to capitalise on.

Eighteen years after they got the opportunity to host the inaugural tournament, the French Rugby League got their wish again in 1972. There were no surprises this time, though: all teams were prepared. France spent the whole year preparing for their shot at World Cup glory.

Their side wasn't full of big names but had the major benefit of playing all their matches at home. They also picked local referees who understood their style of football. To underline their seriousness, former Test captains Antoine Jiminez, Marcel Bescos and Georges Aillères picked the team.

Within the squad, they had sensational winger Serge Marsolan, who scored the tournament's most spectacular try in 1970; veterans such as second-rower Francis de Nadai; centre Michael Moliner; prop Victor Serrano; and exciting debutants like Jacques Franc and Jacky Imbert. Prop Carlos Zalduendo, who later became the president of the French Rugby League, played in his first World Cup tournament.

France started well, winning their first game against New Zealand 20–9, easily outpointing the visitors in the scrums and dominating the kicking duel. That was their high point, though. Despite pushing Australia and Britain reasonably hard, they failed to win any other games, missing a chance at the final they desperately needed. The Kiwis continued to fight hard.

The trouble with tomato sauce

Eighteen-year-old halfback Dennis Williams became the youngest player ever to make his Kiwis debut when he was picked for the 1971 tour to Great Britain and France. He went on to play thirty Tests for the Kiwis spanning more than a decade, including three World Cups and two Australian tours.

When I spoke to Kiwis skipper Roy Christian recently, he vividly remembered a time in New Zealand rugby league history that genuinely promised so much. For a short time, the national side were able to beat the other three major nations regularly. However, on that tour, Williams, like a few of the other players, was a little naïve. Christian explained:

> Going to France was a real eye-opener for the younger players. I will always have fond memories of one particular moment on the trip. Dennis took a stack of tomato sauce with him! He didn't know whether they would have it there. The whole tour was such a unique experience and we really came together as a team.

Rugby league in New Zealand was still an amateur game at that stage and the Kiwis were also up against some of their elite players defecting to Australia, England or France to play on professional contracts. Their player pool was so shallow it was more like a puddle.

Remarkably, New Zealand managed a muddy victory against Australia at Carlaw Park (24–3) and Test series wins in both Britain and France, earning a brief ranking as the top rugby league nation in the world. Those were heady days for a team that had only managed three wins in fifteen World Cup games. Translating that into another consistent year in 1972 proved too difficult with limited resources.

Thinking again about when the Kiwis faced France in the first pool match, Christian had an alternative theory on what might have worked second time around.

I always thought if we played halfback Graeme Cooksley, we might have won. That's no disrespect to Brian Tracey, who was picked in his place. See, the French guys really enjoyed watching Graeme play and were very keen to have him play in their competition as a professional. Thinking about it again, if he was selected, they might have focused on him instead of thinking about the game and themselves. In the end we opted for Brian, as we wanted to use his stronger kicking game. We called Brian 'Little Kiore' [in Maori], or 'Little Mouse', because he was quick and covered a lot of ground quickly.

Rat cunning aside, France managed a fairly comfortable win in the end. It all could have gone so differently for the visitors. Unfortunately, the New Zealanders were 'hamstrung' before they kicked off – thanks to an excitable young prop called Mita Moha. Christian took me through the rest of story.

> We were warming up before the game. Mita was so fired up to play, as he had tried so hard to get on the park for New Zealand and this was his big chance. It was going to be his first Test match. Anyway we did the haka and everyone gave it heaps as always. Not long after the match started, Mita complained of an injury and had to leave the field. It turns out he pulled his hamstring doing the haka!

The combination of injured players (Bob Paul and John O'Sullivan also picked up injuries) and the intensity of so many games in such a short space of time killed off the brave Kiwis' hopes of progressing past pool play for the first time. The tough loss against the Australians took much of their energy; by the time a rampant and rested Britain turned up, it was too much, too soon. Clive Sullivan's men scored eleven tries to five in a high-scoring clash.

The Kiwis had to return home empty-handed again. If the 1950s and 1960s were barren, the 1970s represented a slightly better return. Yet winning eleven out of thirty-seven Tests across that decade is miserable whichever way you look at it, forgetting the high turnover of players and coaches too. They managed wins against Great Britain, France and Wales, but after celebrating their win at Carlaw Park in 1971, long-suffering New Zealand fans had to wait

another twelve years until they could celebrate another
defeat of the Kangaroos.

Selection dramas

The rampant Australians managed to keep the nucleus
of their tournament-winning World Cup team of 1972
together. Langlands and Fulton directed the attack, while
John O'Neill, Arthur Beetson and Gary Stevens provided
the grunt up front. Harry Bath kept his place as coach to try
and win back-to-back tournaments.

They were a well-drilled, professional team who were in
great form.

Fulton lit up the football field like a comet across a dark
sky. His devastating combination of an electric running
game and a fearless approach ensured his side rarely lacked
for energy or direction during his time in the five-eighth's
position. The blond-haired Fulton featured heavily in the
vital pool match between the Aussies and the British, scoring
three tries, including a brilliant chip-and-chase effort that
became one of the talking points of the whole competition.
Being voted the 1970 World Cup Player of the Tournament
didn't seem to be enough for the future Australian coach; he
was hungry for more success.

Young halfback Dennis Ward was an interesting
selection. He originally represented Australia on the two-
Test tour of New Zealand in 1969 but had to bide his time
to achieve national selection again. After leading Manly to
the 1972 premiership, he got his call-up along with Tommy
Raudonikis to play halfback in the World Cup. The ultra-

competitive Raudonikis went on to play in another two World Cups and captained his country in 1973; Ward, however, was preferred in most of the matches during this series.

Great Britain's talent pool had diminished in comparison. Selecting their side from year to year was a case of musical chairs. Veterans Cliff Watson, Dennis Hartley, Malcolm Reilly and skipper Frank Myler were all gone. Brilliant halfback Alex Murphy made his last international appearance on the 1971 tour by New Zealand; his last act was stiff-arming Kiwi, Ken Sterling.

French referee shockers

Top referees nowadays are full-time professionals. They go undergo regular training to simulate match-time demands such as intense physical drills followed by tests of concentration such as separating egg yolks.

Unfortunately for those at the World Cup, some controversial decisions coloured an otherwise commendable set of performances by the men in charge. The Australians in particular had cause to be aggrieved: they had two of their three pool matches filled with big question marks over the referees' decisions.

In Australia's opener against Great Britain, referee Claude Teisseire awarded Britain a try plus the chance to kick another goal – what we now know as a 'seven point try' – the first of its kind in Test history. After winger John Atkinson scored a try, Teisseire walked out to halfway and awarded Britain a penalty kick. He explained that Australian forward

John Elford had attempted a late tackle on Atkinson as the winger went to put the ball down. Everyone was confused, except the referee, who quite rightly pointed out Elford's indiscretion. Britain ended up winning by six points.

Teisseire's ruling was tame compared to what happened during Australia's match against France. This final pool match was a must-win affair for both teams; the winner would play Great Britain in the final; the loser would have to watch from the stands.

The Australians were only a few points ahead when winger Ray Branighan scored what seemed a perfectly legal try. English referee Mick Naughton had no hesitation in awarding it, but he was overruled by touch judge Jo Biou, who decided that Bob O'Reilly's pass to Branighan was forward. It was at this moment things got interesting. French officials informed Biou that a forward pass didn't constitute grounds to overrule the lead referee. After learning this, Biou changed his story and declared Branighan had actually stepped into touch instead. By this stage, everyone was confused, the Australians were getting angry and the match officials continued to argue.

Play was stopped for ten minutes as the referees tried to get their stories straight. The other touch judge colleague threatened to leave the field. Furious, Australia's skipper Graeme Langlands was ready to boycott the rest of the match and walk off the park. Seldom had a rugby league Test match contained this sort of drama before.

Referee Naughton gained control and eventually Australia were awarded the try. It didn't matter in the end:

the visitors won 31–9 and booked a place in the World Cup final a week later. Australian players who took part in that match have different views on what actually happened. Some felt Biou was trying to help France by disallowing a legitimate try. It certainly galvanised the Australians, who were fed up and just wanted to win. They made the final, and with it the right to play Britain.

Great Britain's George Nicholls, the hard-running lock with a famous crunching tackle, remembers his team were massive outsiders to defeat the Kangaroos.

'Going into the World Cup, Australia was the favourite. I had only started my international career a few months earlier and was brought in with Steve Nash and some other new players.' It was a new era for Britain. Despite the changes, both sides had vital men in their forward packs who remained ever-present throughout the 1970s.

At each other's throats

On the pitch, Australia was doing the business. Apart from that tight loss to Britain, the easy victories over France and New Zealand were achieved without much sweat. They were building nicely to take home another World Cup trophy. Despite their accomplishments and winning ways, the biggest problem the Australians faced wasn't a big Nicholls tackle or a Charlton break; it was their own team.

Harry Bath, who became increasingly incensed by the referee's performance, recalls a story that wasn't widely known until many years later. Throughout the two week period in France, trouble was slowly brewing between captain Langlands and team manager Clancy Kingston. This was their third tournament together. The origins of their animosity are still not clear.

They argued and didn't agree on a variety of issues. Bath did his best to smother the problem and keep it away from the other players, but he believed the battle behind the curtain unsettled everyone.

In the end, Bath decided to lock both Langlands and Clancy in a room and demanded that they resolve their differences. It was too late. By that stage, the damage their arguments had caused within the squad couldn't be erased. The constant arguing had destroyed the sense of team harmony built up over the last few years. Bath, a brilliant coach with strong views on man management, decided right then that the 1972 World Cup would definitely be the last time he coached Australia. Before he ended his last shift, a couple of his players decided to test their boss's patience one last time.

Blame it on a night of larrikin behaviour

It was only a few days before the final and the Australian squad was restless. By their thinking, France was the most inhospitable place they could have imagined. That's not to totally dismiss the friendly staff and welcoming atmosphere in the south of France, but Lyon in winter wasn't exactly giving the Australians cause to rub their hands together with excitement. For starters, there wasn't a barbeque for miles.

Forget entertainment – unless you understood French, it was pointless to watch any television – plus the food was too extreme for the players' more simple tastes. Walking wasn't an option either, unless you wanted to show your colleagues what frostbite looked like. Tempers were rising by the day. In short, it felt like prison and even worse, the wardens spoke a different language.

Lock Bob McCarthy remembers a few players were trying to overcome niggling injuries during that week. He'd hurt his ankle and others, like centre Paul Sait, also had knee problems. After the squad finished training in the morning, some of the more senior players decided to take entertainment matters into their own hands.

The Australians started a game of cards. Beer came out shortly afterwards. They continued drinking as the day moved effortlessly into night. It got late. Langlands decided to leave for bed early. McCarthy followed soon after. What happened next sounds like the stuff of legend, but on this occasion, both players verified it as fact.

In the pitch black, McCarthy wandered through the hotel foyer en route to his hotel room. Out of nowhere, a body came flying towards him and crash tackled him to the floor. After getting his bearings, the big lock recovered quickly and proceeded to throw the much smaller offending body across the room like a tissue box, before pummelling it with punches until it refused to move. He knew right then it was Langlands. McCarthy left his skipper and went to bed without knowing how much damage he had caused.

Langlands recalled a similar version of events, blaming the 'wrestle' on boredom. The next morning at breakfast, Bath found out about the punch-up (McCarthy thought a waiter told the coach – but Langland's bruising was plain to see in broad daylight in any case). He was deeply unhappy about what had happened. As punishment, Bath ordered McCarthy, Langlands, Sait and others to run laps of the surrounding area. The running course included concrete, pebbles and other assorted natural surfaces, all designed to teach those who decided to get drunk a big lesson. It didn't end very well. Sait ended up injuring his knee again, and McCarthy had to stop halfway suffering from soreness.

When the Australians turned up three days later to face Britain, they were drained, flat and injured. It may be convenient to say it now, but McCarthy didn't mind: blame Australia's poor World Cup final performance on a night of larrikinism a few days earlier.

Props taking centre stage

Terry Clawson couldn't believe what he was hearing. On Saturday 31 August 1963, right before a big game of rugby league, he had been informed he was highly unlikely to play the sport again. He had contracted tuberculosis, a horrible disease that affected his lungs. Clawson felt he could have caught it while working a few years earlier with a sick colleague. It was a shocking thing to hear.

Despite being as fit and strong as any of his teammates, the big prop was now facing a halt to his career. The prognosis wasn't good: there was a chance that if his body didn't respond to the medication, he could die.

This couldn't be right. Death in your early twenties? A big strong rugby league player like me? Clawson was absolutely devastated. He'd already had fine success as a professional and had debuted for Great Britain earlier that year. Clawson refused to believe the last two years of chronic coughing was anything more than a common cold. Surely his career – and life – couldn't be finished already?

In one of sport's great triumphs, Clawson managed to overcome the vicious disease and went on to play professionally for another seventeen years, retiring at age forty. He played over 600 matches in England and Australia, as well as fourteen Tests for Great Britain.

Nine years after he was diagnosed with tuberculosis Clawson was proud to be selected as one of the thirteen men to represent Great Britain in the 1972 World Cup final. Not only a fine ball-playing forward, Clawson was also the number one goal-kicker and a fine punter of the football in general play. When kicking for goal, he chose to approach the football directly head-on. It was only a couple of years later that players began the 'coming from the side' kicking style.

His story of illness may have been lost on some of his younger teammates, but Clawson's triumph during the World Cup remains to this day the greatest comeback in British sport. Over in the opposition ranks, Australia also had a couple of forwards who inspired.

Prop forwards are traditionally the unsung heroes in any rugby league team. Their job is simple: gain as many metres with the ball as possible. The role involves throwing themselves into the biggest opposition players, ensuring possession and territory is capitalised. In the early 1970s, the concept of interchanging and resting players was still many years off, so the big men had to play the entire game. In that era, the Australians and the British were blessed with some excellent props. Arthur Beetson and John O'Neill had brilliant attacking skills to go with their ability to gain yardage with ball in hand.

Beetson had a large build for a prop during his playing days. At six foot one and weighing over a hundred kilograms, he had the size to stand up in most tackles. You'd be surprised to learn his mates in Roma, Queensland, used to call him 'Bones', as he picked at his food when he was a kid. He was so skinny they thought he might end up as a jockey. But in his early teens, an appendix operation changed everything. He began to grow, as did his appetite. Soon, Beetson's nickname changed to 'Big Artie'.

He'd come a long way before the 1972 World Cup. Taunted by the Australian rugby league media after his Test debut in 1966 as 'Half-A-Game-Artie', he was ridiculed for playing like a demon in the first forty minutes, only to be replaced quickly during the second. But Beetson endeared himself to the public – he was your typical knockabout bloke, slightly overweight, and had a general honesty about him. He went on to play in four World Cups, including captaining Australia for the 1975 tournament.

O'Neill's stamina was enduring, as well as his turn of pace for one of the biggest players on the field. He seized his chance not long after play got underway in the final.

Against the run of play and with Australia on the attack, O'Neill grabbed the ball and in a scooting run sideways, managed to outpace some of the quickest men in the Great Britain side. Gritting his teeth and striding at full length,

O'Neill kept going as if no one could stop him. British fullback Paul Charlton couldn't get there quick enough to stop the rampaging, long-haired O'Neill, who bulldozed his way to the corner for his side's first try. It was a cracking start for the visitors. Little did the unsuspecting crowd know that the Australians had another display of brilliance to come.

Langland's superman effort

Clive Churchill, Australia's champion fullback of the 1950s, wrote in August 1975, '... at his peak Graeme Langlands was magnificent. Real champions prove themselves over a period. Flash-in-the-pans come and go; Langlands has been an outstanding try-scorer and is reliable in defence under pressure. He is my ideal fullback.'

Despite his gifted skillset, Langlands had a fiery and hard-nosed personality. According to his peers, he drove himself beyond normal physical limits and was the most professional player of the 1970s. Operating mostly at fullback, he went on to be the first man to score a hundred points in Anglo-Australian Test matches, a record that will probably never be broken.

He expected nothing less than total commitment from his teammates. It didn't matter if you were tiny or huge, he would tackle you at the same intensity – 120 per cent. Equally, there was nothing given, nothing taken as far as going easy on the paddock was concerned.

Langlands was an athletic machine who had a great turn of pace too. Coupled with his stint as captain-coach of Australia from 1973 to 1975, he was the pre-eminent world footballer of the 1970s. Like all truly great sportsmen, he chose the grandest stage of all to showcase his athletic prowess.

About thirty minutes into the final, Australia was on the attack and led 5–2. Dennis Ward, the eighteen-year-old rookie halfback, launched a towering kick from his team's forty-metre line. What wasn't known, was Langlands and Ward were the only ones who knew about this planned play – not even their teammates were aware.

Langlands anticipated this last play option and had already positioned himself in the attacking line, having moved up from his place at fullback. That's when time froze. Everything paused. At the precise moment the leather football left Ward's boot in anger, the Australian skipper jack-knifed ahead, his eyes only on the heavens. The punt was in the air for a maximum of five seconds, but Langlands had incredible speed and burst ahead of the pack.

As the ball was dropping back to earth, the lanky fullback made his move, jumping forward through the air like an action movie star. He grabbed the ball in mid-air, put the ball down on the ground and somersaulted forward all in one quick moment. It was perfectly executed. Langlands lay there, spreadeagled, collecting his breath. His teammates roared with delight and started the customary post-try celebrations, which in those days involved a fist pump and a pat on the back.

The whole stadium erupted in a huge roar. Spectators screamed in a mixture of disbelief, amazement and excitement. Langlands was simply unbelievable. To move so fast and to have the athletic ability, poise and timing he displayed was something they had never seen before. It certainly seemed out of place in the drab stadium in Lyon.

The Australians gathered themselves, ready to run back and reset for the kick-off. Here's where the controversy started. Referee Georges Jameau ruled immediately Langlands was offside.

Prop forward Arthur Beetson thought the referee simply couldn't believe someone could get there that quickly. He was certain it was a try. Mark Harris was standing right where Ward kicked the ball. 'Changa was behind me when the ball was kicked, and I was behind Wardy. It was a legitimate try, absolutely no doubt about it.'

In the mid-season Test between Australia in New Zealand in 2008 at the Sydney Cricket Ground, Greg Inglis pulled off a stunning move that would be the closest to Langland's effort in the modern era. Inglis hurtled through the air and batted the ball back into the field of play, enabling Mark Gasnier a catch-and-put-down effort for a gravity-defying try. In purely athletic terms, Inglis stands above the rest. But the Australian centre's effort is a distant second to Langland's, especially as there were no protein powders, high performance testing or skinfold tests back then. Langland's feat was truly remarkable.

The moment became part of rugby league and World Cup folklore as 'the greatest try never scored'. Yet the Australians were philosophical about the ruling afterwards; after all, they had chosen Jameau as the lead referee. After watching his counterpart's brilliant efforts, it was the British skipper's turn to change the game not long afterwards.

Sullivan and Nicholls team up

He was just a frail kid with spindly little legs. By his late teens, he required several operations on his knees, feet and shoulders. Doctors told him he wasn't likely to walk again, let alone play contact sport. Then came a near-fatal car crash but even this didn't dent the spirit of the man they called 'Sully'. Clive Sullivan went on to play nearly 600 club matches over twenty years, as well as captaining Great Britain and Wales in two World Cups.

Growing up in the suburb of Splott in Cardiff, Wales, Sullivan played rugby union as a youngster. He was gifted, he had excellent skills, good pace and natural athletic ability, but for a while he escaped the attention of most British clubs, until finally Hull signed him up.

Sullivan's blistering pace helped him gain quick elevation to the national side. He played in three of Britain's fixtures in the 1968 World Cup, scoring a try in the first match against Australia and, in the final game, a 38–14 win over New Zealand in Sydney, he became the first British player to score a hat trick in a World Cup match.

By 1972, Sullivan had become Great Britain's captain. Significantly, he was Britain's first black national sporting captain. He led his team to victory over Australia (27–21), France (13–4) and New Zealand (53–19), claiming a try in each game.

His World Cup teammate George Nicholls enjoyed playing under him. 'I have a lot of respect for Clive. He was a good captain. He was always encouraging to his players, but at the same time gave them a telling off if they deserved it. He treated you well.'

So when the game was in the balance in the World Cup final and Britain needed some inspiration. Come in Nicholls.

Australian centre Mark Harris was carrying the ball up-field dangerously close to the try-line when second-rower Nicholls came flying through the air. With an expertly executed cover tackle, Nicholls knocked the ball free and stopped a crucial try. Nicholls was modest when I mentioned the tackle. He thought nothing of it.

'The final was a great game. Looking back, that cover tackle on Mark Harris was just part of my job.'

Nicholls picked up the smaller Harris and drove him into the ground, a tackle right out of the 'how to win a World

The scars of sport: Mark Harris sports a swollen eye and a bent nose as he lines up to play France in Toulouse.
Rugby League Journal

Cup final' defensive manual. The speed at which he hit Harris, who was probably visualising how good the try would feel, certainly rattled the young centre. Crunching tackles and excellent ball-handling skills became trademarks of Nicholls's career. He was just a rookie when he made Britain's World Cup team, having made his Test debut less than a year before.

If John O'Neill's efforts inspired his captain, then Nicholls' gave his own skipper a huge boost too.

Clive Sullivan was lurking on the side-line in cover defence just as Nicholls went in with his big tackle. The next twenty seconds changed the match and will easily go down as one of the most astonishing and memorable moments of any Test match.

Anticipating an error from Harris, Sullivan swooped in and regathered the ball. From here, it was like watching a gazelle run across savannah. Sullivan suddenly put on a huge sidestep to get clear of any cover defence, swerving to the right, and then accelerated away down the touch-line. The crowd, which was fairly subdued because of the dull exchanges up to that point, seemed to get up out of their seats in unison to watch what happened next.

Sullivan kept running with his high-knee, loping style. He had a ten-metre head start on his opponents, who'd been expecting a try down the other end. The Australians seemed to give up – except one. It was O'Neill, the hero of the hour for his team, who gave chase. His tired legs pumping, a look of steely determination on his face, he chased after the British skipper with all his energy. O'Neill's courage should be remembered in history as much as Sullivan's brilliant run.

The lanky Welshman had too much pace for the Australian, yet O'Neill's valiant refusal to give up – he kept running until Sullivan scored the try – meant he had to score in the corner, leaving Clawson a much harder kick at goal.

Just as opposite captain Langlands was on his haunches after a superb effort a few minutes earlier, Sullivan finished on his knees gasping for air. This time it was a legal try. Britain was back in the contest. Despite the Australian prop's best efforts, Clawson converted from the side-line to give his team an even bigger lead.

Sullivan's try represented many things for not just his team, but all who had followed his career. He was indeed a rare player who had unbridled passion for the game. His wife Rosalyn later remarked that he would have played the World Cup final without pay, such was his love for rugby league. After retiring from Great Britain the following year, Sullivan went on to lead his native Wales in the 1975 World Cup. Unfortunately, this tale doesn't have a happy ending off the field.

Fifteen years later, Sullivan developed cancer. He died aged only forty-two in 1985. As a mark of respect, the City of Hull named the A63 road 'The Clive Sullivan Way'.

Half-time jitters

It could have been the most spectacular moment in World Cup history.

After Ward made a crucial break and passed it to Beetson who was looming in support, twelve British players' heads went down. The big Australian prop had an unmarked passage to the try-line and strolled over, unaware of any dangers that might be lurking. Enter Mike Stephenson, the British hooker.

Stephenson followed Beetson across the try-line and tackled him, desperately trying to knock the ball loose. Luckily, the skilful Australian had the presence of mind to keep his eye on the ball. He shrugged off the British number nine and planted the ball carefully with both hands for a try. A quick conversion meant the Kangaroos had a 10–5 lead.

Stephenson only played six Tests for Great Britain, his debut coming in the 1971 tour at home against the Kiwis. Cunning, with a blond mop that showed signs of premature balding, Stephenson had a professional approach that was just the tonic to keep his team together.

'I felt our build-up for the game was top class. Jim Challinor was a fine coach. He was calm and collected and made us work hard to ensure we operated as a unit.'

An act of courage by one of his team members inspired Stephenson to keep pushing through the pain barrier.

Before they headed out onto the pitch, Stephenson turned to his colleague Steve Nash to discuss last-minute scrum tactics. Blood was trickling down his legs. Nash then showed a wide-eyed Stephenson the three massive boils on his legs. From that moment, nothing would be too tough or painful. It lifted the British boys. By all accounts from different players, Nash didn't complain, and kept going.

With the game in the balance and needing a score from the Lions, captain Sullivan again provided the necessary impetus for his team. He swooped on a loose pass and created room for a teammate, with Stephenson able to score near the uprights. Clawson converted and suddenly the score was locked at 10-all.

The international rules stated that a tied score at full-time would mean another twenty minutes, so the two battle-weary foes had no choice but to continue.

Frantic final minutes

After one hundred minutes of football, both teams couldn't be separated on the scoreboard. In a frantic last stanza of the match, both teams had plenty of genuine chances to win.

Langlands put a huge kick up close to his try-line, but Paul Charlton caught it cleanly and counter-attacked. British centre John Walsh shaped to kick but then stepped through a couple of defenders, running a full twenty metres before passing neatly to Chris Hesketh backing up on the inside. With only the fullback to beat, he kicked ahead to try and regather but was tackled late, ruining his chance of following his kick. Referee Jameau saw it and awarded a penalty to Great Britain, around thirty metres out from the goal post, ten metres in from touch. The Australian captain threw the football at Sullivan in disgust.

Clawson paused, ran in and kicked for goal. It had the length, but missed to the right of the posts.

Moments earlier Branighan had also missed a shot at a drop goal. Great Britain knew that if the scores were tied at the end of the match, they would win as they had a better points for and against during the pool matches. It was the

Clive Sullivan carried by British teammates with the World Cup at Lyon in 1972. The British players are, left to right: Mick Stephenson, Chris Hesketh, Clive Sullivan, Steve Nash (in Australian jersey) and Phil Lowe.

Rugby League Journal

first time a rugby league Test had gone into extra time, let alone the first in a World Cup final.

With Australia using up their tackles, Langlands kicked it down-field. With the ball still aerial, Jameau blew his whistle to signal full-time. It was over. Great Britain had done it again. In a jubilant celebration, Sullivan hoisted the trophy high in the air.

Little did they know it, but this would be the last time Great Britain would win the World Cup.

Were they expecting a ticker-tape parade? Probably not. Perhaps with the tournament being held in deepest France, the British public didn't exactly embrace their national team when they returned home with the trophy. Stephenson remembered disembarking at the airport to be greeted by no one. Only a freelance photographer who was there by chance asked whether they were the Great Britain heroes from France.

As it turned out, goal-kicker Clawson was walking through the arrivals hall with Stephenson and Sullivan, the two try-scorers, and the photographer got the perfect shot.

A huge cost

This story has some unfortunate endings. Centre Geoff Starling – the youngest player ever to represent Australia – at eighteen years, 181 days old in a minor match on tour against New Zealand – was forced to retire only four years later after he developed what would later be confirmed as Addison's disease, a failure of the adrenal gland to produce cortisone.

Today, Kangaroo lock-forward Gary Stevens remembers little if anything of his career from 1970 onwards due to a constant issue with blood clots in his brain. He believes the condition was caused by a collapsed scrum during a Test against Great Britain in the middle of that decade.

World Cup mania

Just two World Cups took place in the 1960s; four took place in the next decade. The World Cups of 1975 and 1977 added to an already full calendar of Test matches. Great Britain split into separate Wales and England sides in 1975, when the tournament was renamed 'The World Championship' and held over months, rather than weeks.

After a close World Cup final in 1977 held in Australasia, the International Federation decided to take stock of the past decade. Four tournaments in seven years meant the public was sick of world championships, it believed. It was not until the mid-1980s that the tournament started again. Unfortunately for the rest of the world, this decade would signal an uninterrupted period of Australian dominance.

Back during the presentations in Lyon, Stephenson remembers looking around and thinking, 'We're world champions.' He moved into broadcasting and the media upon retirement and now calls the Super League and Test matches featuring Great Britain. It must rankle that he was one of the last in a Lions shirt to utter those words. And he might be for some time yet.

There have only been a few extra-time matches in Test match history – the most notable being the 2006 Tri-Nations final between Australia and New Zealand – and none to last the full distance without further scoring.

As Stephenson reflected, there was no ticker-tape parade for the Great Britain team, simply a quiet satisfaction in taking home the big prize. More than forty years later, British rugby league still looks upon that day with huge fondness.

Scoreboard: **Great Britain 10** (Mike Stephenson, Clive Sullivan tries; Terry Clawson 2 goals) drew with **Australia 10** (Arthur Beetson, John O'Neill tries; Ray Branighan 2 goals). Great Britain won due to having a better points differential in pool play.

Match 5, 1988

THE HAKA AND THE HYPE

New Zealand v. Australia

Eden Park, Auckland, New Zealand
9 October 1988
World Cup final

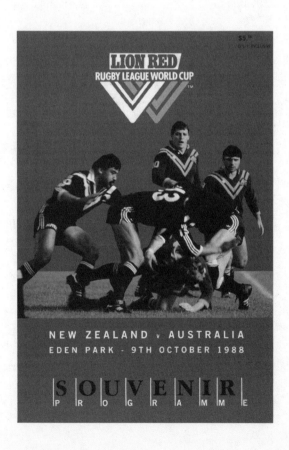

NEW ZEALAND	AUSTRALIA
1. Gary Mercer	1. Garry Jack
2. Tony Iro	2. Dale Shearer
3. Kevin Iro	3. Andrew Farrar
4. Dean Bell (captain)	4. Mark McGaw
5. Mark Elia	5. Michael O'Connor
6. Gary Freeman	6. Wally Lewis (captain)
7. Clayton Friend	7. Allan Langer
8. Adrian Shelford	8. Paul Dunn
9. Wayne Wallace	9. Ben Elias
10. Peter Brown	10. Steve Roach
11. Kurt Sorensen	11. Paul Sironen
12. Mark Graham	12. Gavin Miller
13. Mark Horo	13. Wayne Pearce
Interchange:	Interchange
14. Shane Cooper	14. Terry Lamb
15. Sam Stewart	15. David Gillespie
Coach: Tony Gordon	Coach: Don Furner

Referee: Graham Ainui

As All Blacks captain David Kirk hoisted the inaugural rugby union World Cup high into the air at Eden Park on 20 June 1987, New Zealand could finally point to something tangible for all their decades of supremacy on the international rugby stage. Life was good.

Just a few months later, though, the Wall Street stockmarket crash caused a worldwide economic downturn. New Zealand felt the full effects like everywhere else. But because the mighty All Blacks were world champions, life was somehow a little bit rosier.

Indeed for many people during times of hardship, the feeling of watching their team win a competition can be nothing short of euphoric. Sport is hugely important to New Zealanders' collective psyche. They point to their success on the world sporting stage as a badge of honour, and bask in quiet contentment that whether it be cricket, athletics or rugby union, their shallow pool of a few million people can produce such splendid results. A World Cup tournament is the highest mountain any team can climb.

Kiwi rugby fans can at least count on World Cup tournaments being held every four years. Brazilian soccer player Ronaldo famously said that winning the 2002 FIFA World Cup was better than sex. 'It's not that sex isn't good but the World Cup is every four years and sex is not,' he said. But for rugby league, the World Cup intervals have been as varied as two, three, five and eight years.

After a drawn-out tournament that started in 1985 and took three years to confirm the finalists, New Zealand and Australian rugby league players as well as their fans could at last celebrate their special day. The last World Cup had been held in 1977. Many players began and ended their careers during the interval between World Cups. Wonderful players like Australians John Ribot and Greg Brentnall, New Zealand's Gary Prohm and Shane Varley as well as France's Joel Roosebrouck missed out on the chance to play in a World Cup.

This time, the Kiwis were able to reach their first final after decades of barely being competitive. The Aussies, Brits and French routinely made a mockery of New Zealand's so-called "Big Four" status through regular victories. But the 1980s brought great coaches, a much bigger player pool and an expanded Australian and British club competition. Better yet, the final was to be held in Auckland, the country's rugby league epicentre.

Forget all those years of poor results. According to newspaper columns on both sides of the Tasman, the Kiwis started as favourites against Australia for the first time in history.

The optimism was justified in some areas. Led by inspirational centre Dean Bell, the New Zealanders had players across the park that could compete with their high-profile Australian counterparts. Gary Freeman and Clayton Friend formed a creative and dynamic halves pairing. Forwards Kurt Sorensen and Mark Graham gave the side toughness and commitment, while Adrian Shelford, cousin of future All Blacks great Wayne, always charged with gusto up front.

Auckland got swept up in rugby league fever like it was the only event in town that weekend. Australian Wayne

Pearce was taken aback at how much the locals embraced the World Cup final.

'I remember there was no other sport on in Auckland at that time – it was before cricket and after the rugby union season had finished,' he said. 'There was a massive void that needed to be filled. The World Cup final was it. I remember seeing these big billboards everywhere promoting the game. It was the first time that rugby league had such prominent exposure in New Zealand.'

The match also broke down barriers. People who had never attended a rugby league match were drawn in by the novelty surrounding the event. This wasn't just a league game. For many, it was a significant New Zealand sporting event.

The Kangaroos quietly entered the country. They weren't quite like the Greeks entering Troy inside the Trojan Horse – players of the calibre of Wally Lewis, Dale Shearer and Steve Roach could hardly have gone unnoticed – but the Australians still flew under the radar. They should have given thanks to the local scribes, who proclaimed the Kiwis as the new world number one.

One who tempered his reporting was rookie *New Zealand Herald* reporter Chris Rattue. The World Cup was his first major assignment as a rugby league reporter. He wrote an article featuring former Kiwis great Fred Ah Kuoi, who laughed at the notion that the Kiwis were favourites. Beware of the Australians.

In one of the greatest displays of reverse psychology, Kangaroos coach Don Furner turned the lamp of praise up even further on his opponents: This Kiwis team is the best ever. We are most definitely the underdogs. Australia is really up against it.

The Kiwis, unaccustomed to such lavish praise, lapped it up. The goodwill was like a warm blanket, providing warmth but also blinding them to the task's enormity. This cocoon of comfort would be ripped off as soon as New Zealand prop Peter Brown kicked off in front of a record crowd at Eden Park. The mostly Kiwi supporters had settled in to watch their team exact revenge on their traditional rivals and see their league team match their union team's results.

The Invincibles

Maybe it was selective amnesia. Or perhaps the 47,363 fans at Eden Park that afternoon simply refused to acknowledge Australia's historic achievements six years previously, events that are still talked about in revered terms today.

The Kangaroos had arrived on England's shores in 1982 with a young team and the promise of a new era. Great Britain was intent on revenge for a lop-sided series loss in the 1979 Ashes series. What unfolded was astonishing and set the tone for further decades of Australian dominance.

Johnny Whiteley was well aware of the enormous challenge. When he took over the Great Britain coaching reins in 1980, he could tell very quickly that his side was largely a bunch of unfit, poorly skilled players. They were happy playing within the English club competition and were completely unaware of the advances Australia had made in terms of attitude to fitness. Whiteley understood Great

Britain's team, and played with, captained and coached the side in an association that started in 1954.

> The problem was we were so inferior physically to the Australians. We stayed within our own bubble and parameters and were happy with that. I felt strongly that you must look around the corner rather than staying within the now. We were only interested in ourselves. In English rugby, we had the same talent and ability as Australia, but lacked the regular physicality week in, week out, for each game. We didn't have enough time or effort to lift them to that new horizon that we needed to be in those games [the three Tests in 1982]. The Australians were a wonderful side.

Whiteley asked his squad to run a couple of laps of the oval during the week leading up to the first Test. BBC commentator Ray French had visited the Australian training session during that same week and was so taken by the sheer difference in levels of fitness between the two sides that what happened next came as no surprise. As the players jogged around the oval, Whiteley joined in and, embarrassingly, outpaced them all. Former players sometimes keep themselves fit and the 1954 and 1960 World Cup player was a committed trainer. The problem was, he was fifty, and they were mostly twenty-somethings.

Whiteley is a marvel. Now in his eighties, he still works out six times a week, goes for long runs and operates a gym. When I spoke to him, he was forthright in his opinions, and his passion for British rugby league still ran deep.

Back to the tour. The British public still saw their team through rose-tinted glasses. They had no idea about who these Aussies were. Picked a bunch of no-names, I see! Australia had indeed picked a young side, which was seen as a flawed tactic compared to Great Britain's more experienced-looking team.

The next three Tests stunned the British firstly into silence, then appreciation for the brilliance of the opposition. Crowds were treated to a display of such flair, speed and power that even though their team was hammered to the tune of 99–35 across the series, they stood and applauded the magnificence of this brilliant Australian team.

Wayne Pearce was one of the rookie players. Initially taken to gain experience from the likes of veteran lock Ray Price, by the end of the series, he had cemented his place as a regular and a superstar in the making.

The Kangaroo tour of 1982 was a really exciting time for me. It was actually my first trip overseas too. The selectors took 28 players on tour and I was selected as backup lock-forward for Ray Price. Frank Stanton [Australia's coach] ended up selecting me for a couple of the warm-up games ahead of the first Test, which went well. He then selected me for the First Test and I got Man of the Match, eventually getting selected for all three Tests. I was named the Players' Player of the Tour – it was an amazing honour, as that was the only official award we had on tour.

It was an amazing experience. We had a mixture of players who had toured previously, as well as a group of emerging guys who were going to be the next superstars. The likes of Peter Sterling, Mal Meninga, Gene Miles and heaps more toured. It was wonderful.

The calm lasted until half-time in the first Test. Then, leading 10–4, the Kangaroos scored four tries in ten minutes – a period frightening in its display of skill and which reduced Great Britain's team and management to a blubbering mess. Full-time: a 40–4 footballing massacre. Only two British players were retained for the second Test. Five-eighth Brett Kenny (who kept the exceptional Wally Lewis out of the squad) and Pearce made their debuts, while Mal Meninga, Kerry Boustead and Steve Rogers also made huge impressions. Australian rugby league had come a long way.

The virtuoso performance left the British commentators to raid their superlatives bin.

'Move it wide. Where too? The Australians are moving up so quickly.'

'Meninga hands him off like he's a little boy.'

'It's too easy.'

Forwards Rod Reddy, Les Boyd and Craig Boyd were able to regularly stand in tackles and offload the football. Players ran with numbers in support and swarmed quickly in defence. They produced spectacular set plays in attack with ease. Big centre Mal Meninga was deemed a surprise selection, but like many, he launched his international career that day. He had a devastating mixture of pace, power and accurate goal kicking that proved too much for a shocked Great Britain team.

Wally Lewis later gave credit to his coach Frank Stanton.

> Frank was determined right from the start of the tour to
> keep the players in line – discipline was his key word.
> On the back of this, we managed to keep our discipline
> for each game. It helped that we were a happy team unit,
> everyone got along well.

Phil Larder, the newly appointed director of the British Amateur Rugby League Association, saw the writing on the wall early and decided to do the unthinkable: contact the enemy and ask for help. It would be an awkward phone call nowadays but was tolerated for the good of international football back then. Larder rang Stanton and asked if he could attend one of his training sessions, as he felt Britain's methods were antiquated. To his credit, Stanton obliged and gave him permission to watch a whole week of training.

Larder was shocked by what he saw. He'd never laid eyes on tackle shields before. Players were running into each other, catching and passing, turning and offloading to find gaps in a defensive line. Following the visit he made a trip to Australia to gain more information. Larder visited various Australian clubs and spoke to former Test great Arthur Beetson, master coach Jack Gibson and Queensland's State of Origin team. Another trend emerged: half the training sessions usually focused on defence. It was a glimpse into the future.

Larder presented his findings to all twenty-two British clubs. The truths hit hard. Australians were very fit yet only trained three times per week and were not full-time professionals. The British players didn't train under match conditions for fear of injury, whereas Australians used cushioned shields and simulated the real game as much as they could. Great Britain was so far behind it would be decades before they would catch up.

State of Origin and Stanton's secrets

Alongside the abundance of coaches and new training methods, the injection of sponsors' money was also a huge fillip for the Australian game. Cigarette giant Rothmans signed on as Australian rugby league's key commercial sponsor in 1982, a deal worth $850,000 over three seasons. State of Origin was also introduced to revive interest in the game in Queensland, who were still fighting for recognition against the dominant New South Wales system. Now, the likes of Wally Lewis, Mal Meninga and Paul Vautin could take on the might of New South Wales; it was the little guy against the establishment. It was a massive coup for Australian administrators, who more than thirty years later still use 'Origin' as their key marketing push.

After Origin came into affect, Stanton established a national coaching scheme that gave Australia a rocket-propelled boost into a rugby league galaxy far ahead of any other country. He was a huge fan of American gridiron and after returning from research missions to America, he brought back technology that would change how rugby league coaches would prepare their teams. This new equipment, such as video recorders, allowed teams to get a real advantage over their opponents.

Stanton was ahead of his time in other areas too. Before the 1982 tour to Great Britain and France, he ran psychoanalysis tests for all his players, analysed their strengths and weaknesses and matched the most compatible roommates together too.

Over a three-month period, he calculated the average tackle count in the Winfield Cup for each position, from fullback to lock-forward, and challenged his players to better those figures. It was intrinsic motivation wrapped into a competition. Stanton dared his team to be the best they could be as individuals, which paid huge dividends as a collective. Having gathered this data for the Winfield Cup, the Kangaroos already had stacks of information about themselves, as well as about Britain and France. Stanton deemed these techniques and preparation crucial to attain victory at Test level. The days of showing up and doing some drills were over.

While these two teams fought for the Ashes, the Kiwis were quietly building a team of their own that could mount a serious challenge.

From a Lowe to a high

The venue: Lang Park in Brisbane. The scenario: rookie Kiwis coach Graham Lowe's second Test in charge. Australia had just returned from their record-breaking trip to Britain and France. Now, in mid-1983, the Kiwis were about to get their own thrashing from this superb Kangaroos team. Or so everyone thought.

Yet Lowe was the complete package. More than just a very good motivator and tactician, he injected the key missing ingredients into his Kiwi teams: preparation, belief and discipline.

Lowe felt New Zealand players suffered a huge inferiority complex when up against Australia. By his reckoning, rather than tackling the Australians, his players were just as likely to ask for an autograph. The coach knew he had players with ability around him, but he needed to get them onside.

Dean Bell, who was in the early stages of his Test career, remembered:

> We had a lot of one-sided games until Graham was
> coach. That year – 1983 – was a turning point – he gave
> us self-belief. I don't think previous New Zealand players
> had any belief we could beat the likes of Australia. But
> Graham gave us good preparation. He made a point of
> saying they bleed, they get hurt like anyone else, and
> they were just regular players. Psychologically, he really
> got into the minds of his players. He gave us a good
> chance of winning.

Preparation almost went off the rails, though, as his team nearly didn't make the venue on time.

John Coffey and Bernie Woods' book *The Kiwis: 100 Years of International Rugby League* recounts this hilarious incident. Lowe scheduled two mini-buses: one for the forwards, one for the backs. The forwards managed to get to Lang Park without any issues, but when the second bus started its journey, things started to go wrong. Physio Glenn Gallagher was acting as driver and quickly realised they were almost out of fuel. Coach Lowe had no time for such trivial matters and had mapped out a strict timetable. The stadium was in sight when a stream of rugby league fans crossed the road en masse, leaving Lowe furious, who reportedly shouted at Gallagher, 'Keep driving, don't bloody stop, they're only *&^% Australians!' The mini-bus eventually arrived, running on empty.

Twenty-two years later, James Leuluai revealed why the bus was nearly empty of fuel – he and Fred Ah Kuoi had taken the bus out during the day and forgot to check the fuel gauge when they returned it.

Two hours before the match, Lowe's legendary motivational skills came to the fore. He showed his team video clips of the New Zealand Olympic gold-winning medal rowers crying tears of joy, and challenged his players to reach a similar level of achievement. It was a brilliant tactic.

Propelled by the sense of togetherness on the training paddock, the New Zealanders carved out a superb 19–12 win and stopped the Australian's seventeen-game winning streak. Dean Bell was delighted. 'It was only my second Test match. [The win] was a pretty huge achievement; it was hugely significant. What happened that night will always remain with me.'

The Kiwis built on the win with an excellent 3–0 series whitewash of Great Britain. In two short years, New Zealand had started to form a core group of world-class players: the likes of skipper Mark Graham, Kurt Sorensen, James Leuluai and Fred Ah Kuoi.

Graham noticed the change in performance and attitude. An experienced captain with Otahuhu, North Sydney and the Kiwis, he felt the tide starting to turn as early as 1978, when Kiwis coach Ces Mountford introduced young talent into the team. Now, Graham felt Lowe's professionalism and meticulous approach to planning improved the Kiwis' competitiveness by four or five levels. By the middle of 1980, New Zealand was playing at their peak – there was a real sense of togetherness and camaraderie – and they wanted to win for their coach.

It was also around this time that international rugby league administrators decided to bring back the World Cup series. Test programs continued as normal and, in a head-scratching decision that confused players as well as fans, certain games were pre-selected as World Cup matches and carried competition points. Papua New Guinea joined France, Australia, Great Britain and New Zealand in the new tournament, which was to be spread across three years and five countries, finishing in 1988.

The 1985 Kiwis had a strong series but lacked the polish to win the first two Tests. After leading for most of the second Test match, a last-minute try by Kangaroos winger John Ribot sank their chances. New Zealand players were downcast; to add to it all, centre Dean Bell suffered a knee injury in the second half. It was down to the third and final Test in Auckland. This is where Lowe really came into his own with his coaching.

'I vividly remember Lowe asking us to take a walk up Queen Street [Auckland's main street] with the rest of the team during the day. The public really got in behind us; there was lots of cheering and people giving their support.'

Lowe's masterstroke worked. This simple idea galvanised the Kiwis and made them determined not to let the final Test slip. The result: an 18–0 victory. Rarely had a New Zealand team put in such a dominating performance over an Australian side; it was the first time the Kangaroos had been held scoreless playing against the Kiwis. Luckily for the New Zealanders, the game carried World Cup points.

As well as having to endure a humiliating defeat and an opening World Cup game loss, the Australians were facing another a much bigger problem: themselves.

Not mate versus mate

Watching Wally Lewis and his teammates band together in the 1988 World Cup final, you wouldn't have guessed the Australian rugby league team was close to imploding three years earlier. Lewis remembers that as the low point in his Test career.

'The 1985 touring side to face New Zealand was the only side where there wasn't any team harmony. It wasn't a happy side; there wasn't a happy relationship between a number of players,' says Lewis.

Queensland had just won that year's State of Origin series, yet the Australian team was dominated by New South Wales players. It was very difficult to get the two sides to mix together, you know. I felt there was a big resentment from the Queensland players towards the New South Wales guys. I didn't handle it all as well as I should have. Either way, changes needed to be made.

Even though the Australians won the first two matches, they only scraped through by the barest of margins (four and six points respectively). Their rising frustration was characterised by the infamous side-line brawl between Greg Dowling and Kevin Tamati in the second Test at Lang Park. After being sin-binned, they continued to have a running discussion as they walked off the field before both players started throwing a flurry of punches. The crowd rose, thinking it was all part of the spectacle, but it underlined how unhappy the Kangaroos were underneath their poor performance. Beneath it all, Australia was collapsing internally. Says Lewis:

We won the first two and were beaten in game three. I remember there were four changes for the final Test and all were Queenslanders. We were lucky not to be beaten by 30. It was a disgraceful performance. There was a perceived controversy with Terry Fearnley [Australian coach] and I not liking each other. Well, that was no secret – I think we hated each other. It was a shame really because that brought out the Queensland versus New South Wales part in an Australian team.

The Daily Telegraph reported that a need for 'more inventiveness and flair' was the reasoning behind these changes. Queensland Rugby League boss Ron McAuliffe, never one for mincing his words, spelled out his thoughts clearly in front of a packed media conference: 'It is a football assassination beyond all reasoning. And there can be no acceptable excuse for it.' It said a lot for the skill of the individuals within the Australian team that they were able to overcome the infighting.

Don Furner replaced Fearnley for the 1986 season as the Australians eyed a return trip to Great Britain, plus a series against a buoyant New Zealand side. The Australians were bloodied and beaten up, ready for the finishing.

The Unbeatables

The year 1986 promised so much for the Kiwis – yet it would end with the emergence of one national coach and the sacking of another. The team were enjoying Lowe's steadying influence and a growing talent pool with experience in the Australian and English competitions. Mark Graham, Clayton Friend, James Leuluai, Dean Bell and Kurt Sorensen all held important roles with professional clubs.

Lowe went in confident ahead of the visiting Australian series that year, but the Kiwis underperformed, losing 3–0. For the first time during his tenure, his position was under scrutiny. Then came a watershed moment that caused confusion and disillusionment for many inside New Zealand rugby league circles. Lowe said he got an offer to continue as Kiwis coach; however, he wanted to coach Wigan at the same time. After administrators initially said yes, they changed their minds and said no. It was all a bit murky.

The end result: Lowe ended his association as New Zealand coach and players were left fuming. Two of the Kiwis' most experienced and best players – Olsen Filipaina and Mark Graham – quit Test football in protest.

Conversely, Australia marched on under Furner's successful leadership. The British public were very excited about the prospect of another series with the exciting Kangaroos, who'd made such an impact in 1982.

The Brits were desperate to reap the benefits of all their work since the last tour. The Rugby Football League introduced professional coaching qualifications, fitness testing, video analysis and coaching programs, all in a bid to try and match the Australians. Four years wasn't enough time though.

This was a hardened Kangaroos team. Team harmony was at its greatest during the series, which says a lot for Don Furner's approach and ability to turn the culture around less than a year after taking charge. Lewis again:

> I still say the '86 side was something else. As the old saying goes, on tour, at least two blokes wouldn't like each other. For that trip – every single bloke got on. The way they mixed it was quite extraordinary. I had a great working relationship with Don too. We set high standards that are still going today.

The British public was excited. So was David Oxley, the British Rugby Football League chairman. Just as the Australians touched down in London, he proclaimed:

The 1982 Kangaroos made such an enormous impact on the British sporting public. I've never known a tour by an overseas team that has been awaited so eagerly as the 1986 Kangaroos. It's going to be a tremendous series ahead of us.

British excitement turned to horror. The first Ashes Test brought in 50,583 fans, a record for a Test match in Great Britain. The home team were more expansive but still went down 38–14. Not much changed throughout the rest of the tour as Australia went through Britain and France unbeaten yet again, gaining the 'Unbeatables' tag.

Luckily for Great Britain, this tour unearthed some great talent who would form the nucleus of their team for the next decade. Ellery Hanley, Garry Schofield, Martin Offiah and Andy Goodway all left great impressions on the Australians, who would later recruit Hanley, Schofield and Offiah for their own club competition.

Henderson's boogie

Ah, the 1980s. There were still characters and big personalities in rugby league back then. Henderson Gill was one of these. His performance for Britain in the third Ashes Test at the Sydney Football Stadium in 1988 produced brilliance as both a player and an entertainer, encapsulating what the game has to offer.

The match was supposed to be a meaningless encounter, as Australia had hammered Great Britain in the first two Tests, leaving this one as a dead rubber. Yet the game carried

World Cup points and the visitors suddenly had more than just pride to play for.

A spirited Britain led 10–0 at half-time, only for Australia to hit back with two tries early in the second half. Leading 16–12 with twenty minutes to go, British centre Paul Loughlin zigzagged his way through a sliding Australian defence and shot away up-field. Gill loomed on the outside and accepted Loughlin's pass with thirty metres to go, out-sprinting Kangaroos fullback Garry Jack on the outside to score an energetic, length-of-the-field try that brought all the British fans out of their chairs to celebrate.

After diving over to score, Gill got up and started twirling his hips, pointing his finger in the air, and did a little dance. Commentator Daryl Eastlake memorably described it as 'a bit of a boogie,' as the stocky winger was embraced by jubilant teammates. It was Britain's first win in sixteen starts against the green and golds, their first in fourteen years on Australian turf. Next stop: Christchurch for a World Cup semi-final.

Gill told reporters after the match, 'I'm really happy. No disrespect to Australia, but the better team won on the day. Rugby league in England has improved.' He was right.

The captaincy issue

Former Kiwis player Anthony Gordon had made his mark as new Kiwis coach in 1987 in many ways. The most significant was replacing Mark Graham as captain.

Graham had been New Zealand's skipper since 1980, as well as captaining Otahuhu in Auckland and North Sydney in the Winfield Cup. He was a key figure in New Zealand's emergence as a genuine power. His success paved the way for other local players to play overseas.

The hugely promising Hugh McGahan was seen as Graham's natural successor at lock and was appointed captain in the mid-season Test against Australia in Brisbane. This match remains one of New Zealand's greatest sporting moments.

Australia fielded a strong team, with Garry Jack, Michael O'Connor, Brett Kenny and Dale Shearer in the back-line, and Lewis and Peter Sterling in the halves. Gordon's new team contained six players who hadn't played against Australia before; debutants included nineteen-year-old centre

Mark Graham was a key figure for the Kiwis throughout the 1980s.
Photosport

Kevin Iro and second-rower Mark Horo; Graham had been dropped from the side. The Kangaroos had racked up ten consecutive wins since their loss to the Kiwis in 1985 and were expected to brush aside the rookie coach and his team.

The Kiwis started very nervously, which was exacerbated when Australia scored a try inside five minutes. Super-fit Sam Stewart's weaving run and pass to Ross Taylor got New Zealand level. Then came the decisive try that broke the Kangaroos. McGahan passed quickly to Bell who powered forty metres up-field, firing a no-look pass to winger Gary Mercer, who stepped his way past Shearer to score. Mercer was one of the new boys, playing his second Test and wasn't even signed to a professional club. His brilliant sidestep became a sought-after commodity soon afterwards. The final score was New Zealand 13, Australia 6.

After the historic win, Graham met with the New Zealand Rugby League several times in 1987 to talk about a possible return to the side. He eventually took to the field in 1988 to face Papua New Guinea and was named vice-captain by coach Gordon.

When McGahan was injured and couldn't take his place in the team for the World Cup final in 1988, Dean Bell was appointed captain even though Graham was easily the most experienced skipper. Bell admitted Graham's selection in the team while not being captain created a big problem in the final.

Mark was a senior player and was the regular New Zealand captain. When I got told I was the new captain, it was pretty sudden. It was an awkward situation [with Graham there also]. That's not to say I wasn't very proud to receive the honour.

For his part, Graham immediately noticed a different culture. He felt the Kiwis had lost a lot of the light-heartedness of Lowe's reign. Now, there were no pranks, no fun; it was all very serious. As a result, the team lacked camaraderie, he thought.

Perhaps it just came down to a difference of opinion, but what's certain is that the Kiwis' success in 1987 created great hope and excitement for what was to come: knockout football.

A cold semi-final in Christchurch

Bell had played rugby league in some uncomfortably cold climates, like Wigan, Leeds and Canberra. Yet when I spoke to him almost thirty years later, he firmly believed the World Cup conditions at the semi-final in Christchurch against the Lions were easily the worst he'd ever experienced in his career.

It was so cold. I always remember right after we won, we felt relief at the game finishing. We just wanted to get off the field. Celebrations were very muted. Unless you were out there on the field, you wouldn't realise how cold it was. There was a southerly wind coming up from the Antarctic. It was just miserable.

Afterwards in the changing sheds, we weren't celebrating either – we just tried to spend that

time getting warm. I remember all these blokes
shivering in the dressing rooms. My other vivid
memory was the showers – we turned them on and
they were cold too!

Britain scored after just two minutes. Despite a few penalty goals by both teams, it was a very even affair. Replacement halfback Gary Freeman's two tries either side of half-time swung the game the Kiwis' way. The visitors managed surge after surge in the final twenty minutes, yet New Zealand's defence held resolute. It was outstanding, committed and disciplined football played in appalling weather. Great Britain had their chances with the boot too – but David Stephenson missed three goals. The Kiwis hung on for a 12–10 win and were into their first ever World Cup final. It had taken thirty-five years.

Hubris and the haka

Mark Graham was a worried man as New Zealand prepared for the most significant game in their history.

He expanded on why in his autobiography, published a year after the World Cup final.

Firstly, he felt by selecting Bell as skipper coach, Gordon put far too much pressure on him and ignored his lack of captaincy experience. Most crucially, the New Zealand team management disregarded the importance of a captain's role.

Secondly, Graham was amazed at the lack of any game plan leading into the match. The team had not gone into any fundamentals about how they were going to play the match.

Australia played a warm-up match against an invitational side and put in a poor performance, which reinforced his feeling that the New Zealanders were in a comfortable space. They could get away with playing however they liked.

Looking back, both Bell and Graham thought too much emphasis had been put into the haka during the week of the final. A number of players were becoming more concerned that the pre-game ritual wasn't as crisp as it should be than with their actual playing preparation.

Bell now knows things went over the top with the hype and the haka practice.

> On reflection, we spent time practising the haka at the expense of preparation. We got ambushed and were carried away by all the hype. I learnt a huge lesson from that week – never to get carried away. The Australians were really professional and set us up – they talked us up as much as the New Zealand media did.

The young skipper would later use that harsh lesson to become one of the game's most respected captains.

But that lay a few years in the future. Now, after the haphazard training sessions, team meetings and player preparation, a very anxious Bell led the Kiwis onto Eden Park as almost 50,000 fans roared in anticipation.

The King returns

Wally Lewis is widely regarded as one of the greatest Australian players of all time. He captained his country on twenty-three occasions and eventually played thirty-four Tests, including two tours of Great Britain and France. He was named in the Kangaroos' team of the century.

Yet it was his deeds for Queensland against New South Wales in the newly formed State of Origin series that put an exclamation mark on his career. Those deeds led to Lewis being awarded a Member of the Order of Australia in 1987, receiving the moniker, 'The King', and having a bronze statue of his likeness placed outside Lang Park. In the Test arena, Lewis was able to draw upon his vast experience during the intense Origin contests. If Bell was nervous, Lewis seemed a man at ease with himself and his team.

Only in Australia could a man be hated as much as he was loved. In an ironic twist that New Zealand fans found hilarious, because of Lewis' passion for donning the maroon of Queensland, he was booed whenever he played a Test match in Sydney. Some say he was a natural showman when on the field; others felt he was just a passionate, very competitive human being who enjoyed playing football for his state and country. Lewis became a rallying force for Australia and the Queensland sides through his inspirational performances on the field. He also helped Australia move on from the politically-charged team selections in the 1980s and got them performing as a group.

Lewis was a creative genius with the ball in hand, a fiery competitor who never took a backward step. He is still a proud ambassador for rugby league today. His induction into the Australian Hall of Fame in 1987 was as much about his contribution to rugby league in general as it was about reviving interest in the game through club, Origin or Test matches. Many in the Eden Park stands may have turned out regardless of who was in the Australian team; yet Lewis was undoubtedly a drawcard by himself. New Zealand crowds appreciated his abilities.

Losing the plot

Forget the magic wins against Australia in '83, '85 and '87; the Kiwis fell flat in their worst performance in a decade. And they did it on the biggest stage.

Eden Park shook with joy as Peter Brown kicked off and the Kangaroos got first use of the football. After a couple of hit-ups, Lewis made a mistake that could have been very costly. Hooker Ben Elias wobbled a poor pass to his captain and Lewis fumbled it. Eden Park was heaving with excitement. The newspapers couldn't have written it any better: Australia knocks on, just twenty seconds gone, New Zealand with a scrum-feed only twenty metres out.

However, the Kiwis conceded a penalty through an incorrect feed in the scrum and Australia was out of danger. It was a pattern that would continue throughout the whole afternoon: Kiwi mistake, Kangaroo attack. From the ensuing set of six tackles, Lewis launched a high kick that found space in front of Kiwis fullback Gary Mercer – who was nursing a shoulder injury – and bounced up for Australia to get another chance with the football. It was a panicky start. It would get worse.

After a few more calm plays, the Australians then cranked up their brilliance in a set move that left the crowd stunned. You had to marvel at the beauty and professionalism of its execution. After a tap penalty, a series of criss-cross passes between forwards and backs left young halfback Allan Langer with an untouched stroll to the try-line. The Kiwi players could only stand and watch. Lewis supplied the final pass and was delighted with his team's confident start. It was pure, clinical stuff by those wearing the green-and-gold.

It was way too easy for the visitors. Australia successfully kicked a couple of penalty goals early and now led 10–0 after a simple conversion.

What was happening in the New Zealand camp? Nothing much, as Bell remembered. When things weren't working out, he didn't know what to say. He felt alone and exposed. What do I do? His lack of captaincy experience showed. As a result, his teammates were running around like a pack of goats in a paddock.

Nothing looked illegal. But on closer viewings, the Kiwis seemed like they were trying to get back into the match by taking it physically to the Australians. Big tackles. Putting extra men in defence. In his autobiography, Gary Freeman disagrees about theories involving rough tactics. Bell thought there was too much. Either way, the tactics seemed disjointed. By contrast, the cool, calm and focused Australians were content with doing the hard work with their forwards, kicking and chasing to try and force a mistake. New Zealand persisted with one-out runners and an over-reliance on their backs doing the hard work. It was upside-down footy – and it wasn't going to work.

Ben Elias potted a drop goal to grab an 11–0 lead after only ten minutes. The Kiwis already had to score three times to overtake the Australians, who had hardly broken a sweat.

Lewis was having a strong impact on the match. He was kicking well and directing their attack. With less than twenty minutes gone, disaster struck the Australian skipper in the shape of Tony Iro's shoulder.

Lewis went for a head-on tackle on Iro, who was playing his first Test match. Replays would confirm he went in with a swinging arm that collected Iro's shoulder. Lewis immediately clutched his arm. He'd broken it. He remembers:

> I knew I had done it straight away. Our trainer came
> on and put a newspaper along my arm, then strapped it
> up. It was the one game I was thinking about for three
> years, so I was devastated. I wanted to stay on as long as
> I could. Not long afterwards, I went to throw a pass and
> it went to the ground, I put it down.

Lewis battled through the pain barrier for another twenty minutes before he was replaced by Canterbury halfback Terry Lamb at half-time.

'He was a pleasure to play alongside during the 1986 Kangaroo tour,' says Lewis. 'We had a slick unit on the bench. It contained a few blokes from Canterbury who were the in-form Sydney team. I had complete faith in Terry to do the job.'

Wally Lewis, with broken arm, holds the World Cup aloft at the end of the 1988 final. Rugby League Journal

So did the rest of the Australians. They added another two tries and reached a scarcely unbelievable 21–0 at the break. The Kiwis were shot. The Kangaroos knew they had done enough. The crowd were shocked.

There was complete silence in the New Zealand dressing rooms at half-time. Graham tried to inject some enthusiasm into the changing sheds, which resembled a hospital waiting room. Australia's huge lead was mentioned. Would you rather be 100–0 down instead? Out in the stands, the spectators were trying to come to terms with what had just happened over the last forty minutes. It was becoming a night to forget.

Australian fullback Dale Shearer capped off an excellent match by scoring right after half-time. The scoreboard was now 25–0. The Kiwis managed a couple of late tries in the second half to Kevin and Tony Iro that only made the scoreline look more respectable. Australia closed out the match easily. No mistakes. That was to be the catch-cry throughout the game. Ray Warren mused in the commentary box that the Kiwis wanted to fight rather than play football.

Lewis held the World Cup trophy aloft with one hand, his broken arm wrapped in a white bandage. After an eleven-year hiatus, one of Australia's greatest got a chance to play in a World Cup final. For hooker Ben Elias it was a sweet return to Test football; his last had been Australia's 18–0 loss against the Kiwis in 1985.

A very public inquisition

Bell's downcast expression said it all as he accepted his runner-up medal from New Zealand Prime Minister David

Lange. Gary Freeman, Clayton Friend and Mark Graham were similarly dispirited. But that's not where the pain ended. Forget the impact of a rampaging Steve 'Blocker' Roach running full tilt. What the senior New Zealand players had to endure afterwards ranks as one of the more divisive moments in New Zealand sporting administration.

NZRL chairman George Rainey was extremely unhappy about the Kiwis' performance and released a report into why they performed so poorly. Rainey questioned the perceived lack of leadership during the game, singling out particular players for special criticism. Many players didn't react well to this.

During a radio interview, Rainey stood by his decision, saying he felt the New Zealand people had a right to understand what went wrong given the Kiwis could have beaten Australia on the day. New Zealand were scheduled to face Australia in three Tests the following July, so he didn't want the side to make the same errors again.

'I can understand some of the players reactions – they are human reactions,' Rainey says. 'Nevertheless, the people leaving the park have talked about two issues from the game: a general lack of leadership and ability of players to coordinate their game, and the rough play instigated by a small number of the players.'

It was a bold move and typified Rainey's firm belief in his approach to the job.

Rugby league writer Chris Rattue remembers it a different way: 'Rainey simply calling a report in the first place pissed a lot of people off. Players didn't have respect for the administration. To do what Rainey did was the final nail in the coffin [for that NZRL administration.]'

Rainey was one of the truly great sporting administrators, Rattue says. He, along with Australia's Ken Arthurton and England's Maurice Lindsay, did great things for international rugby league. No one could question his absolute passion for the betterment of New Zealand rugby league. But publicly asking for a report seemed the wrong decision at the time, judging by players' reactions.

Dean Bell seriously questioned whether his Test career was over. He came back for the 1989 tour of Europe but decided the 34–0 defeat of France in December would be his last Test. He was only twenty-seven. He still has no regrets over retiring so early.

Mark Graham retired from international football after the World Cup final. He was sick of how the selectors refused to take the blame and shifted it squarely onto the players. In his autobiography, he remembered feeling 'mutilated, decapitated and assassinated'.

The Kiwis showed the world their great potential. Although they flopped on the biggest stage, they had eyeballed Australia and Great Britain and managed to topple them on multiple occasions during the decade. If the 1980s invigorated international rugby league, the 1990s would almost destroy it.

Scoreboard: **Australia 25** (Langer 2, Dunn, Roach, Miller, Shearer tries; O'Connor 4, Elias goals) defeated **New Zealand 12** (Kevin Iro, Tony Iro tries; Brown 2 goals) at Eden Park. Crowd: 47,363.

Match 6, 1992

JUMPING AHEAD
OF THE PACK

Great Britain v. Australia

Wembley Stadium, London, England
24 October 1992
World Cup final

GREAT BRITAIN	AUSTRALIA
1. Joe Lydon	1. Tim Brasher
2. Alan Hunte	2. Willie Carne
3. Gary Connolly	3. Steve Renouf
4. Garry Schofield (captain)	4. Mal Meninga (captain)
5. Martin Offiah	5. Michael Hancock
6. Shaun Edwards	6. Brad Fittler
7. Deryck Fox	7. Allan Langer
8. Kevin Ward	8. Glenn Lazarus
9. Martin Dermott	9. Steve Walters
10. Andy Platt	10. Mark Sargent
11. Denis Betts	11. Paul Sironen
12. Phil Clarke	12. Bob Lindner
13. Ellery Hanley	13. Bradley Clyde
Interchange:	Interchange:
14. John Devereux	14. David Gillespie
15. Alan Tait	15. Kevin Walters
16. Kelvin Skerrett	16. John Cartwright
17. Richard Eyres	17. Chris Johns
Coach: Malcolm Reilly	Coach: Bob Fulton

Referee: Dennis Hale

It wasn't quite in the same league as Nike's 'Just Do It' slogan, but the Rugby Football League's advertising campaign to promote the 1992 World Cup final still had a lasting impact on sports fans in London. It helped that England had hosted one of the most famous and best attended Test series in history only two years earlier, with more than 133,000 people flowing through the turnstiles.

In the late 1980s and early 1990s, one man made rugby league fun again: Martin Offiah. His photo was plastered across London's Underground station walls during the week of the final. Above the picture of Offiah, who appeared to leave flames in his wake as he fled the invisible Australian enemy, was the question, 'Will the Aussies catch Offiah at Wembley?' Such a caption, which invoked genuine intrigue about the winger's extreme pace, remained in the minds of many who saw it, some recalling the advert vividly more than twenty years later. Offiah was rugby league's answer to Sonic the Hedgehog, who coincidentally appeared in his first video game in 1991. Both were marketed as 'the fastest thing alive'.

Offiah was just what British rugby league needed. He brought excitement, charisma and extraordinary skills to the game. Hull coach Brian Smith felt that Offiah stood out from any other winger in the competition due to his impact. One of the most prodigiously talented players of all time, Tom Vollenhoven, thought Offiah, at even 75 per cent fit, was still the fastest player going around.

On account of this extreme pace, the English media anointed the Widnes player 'Chariots' after the film *Chariots of Fire*. He could run 100 metres in 10.8 seconds — nothing to challenge Usain Bolt, sure — but it was the manner at which he outpaced and outflanked every opponent he faced that excited crowds and teammates alike.

Offiah was single-handedly responsible for bringing in a new audience to watch league: children. They loved his theatrics and heroics on the pitch, dancing with him as he crossed for a try. Kids swamped the in-goal area whenever the six foot winger crossed over, embracing his enthusiasm for the game. Offiah was a natural showman who got his pleasure out of thrilling big audiences. He even gave up rugby union in his early days because he was sick of playing in front of paltry crowds. Offiah desperately wanted to be the finisher, the one who got all the glory. Beneath the showmanship,

Martin Offiah in a typical action shot: on his way to score another try.
RLPhotos.com

he had immense belief in his abilities. He quickly rattled up points; forty-two tries in his debut season, fifty-eight in his second; two tries on Test debut. English rugby league hadn't seen anything like it since Billy Boston. Great Britain coach Malcolm Reilly quickly fast-tracked him into the Test team.

While Offiah was leaving commentators struggling for superlatives, the Australians had a superb winger of their own. Andrew Ettinghausen – or 'ET' to his mates – made his international debut in the same year and shaped up to be Offiah's number one nemesis in the World Cup final. It was during the 1992 Ashes series that the battle of these two lightning-quick players reached its zenith.

Early in the first Test, Offiah got the ball in space with seventy metres to travel. He easily passed Allan Langer and only had one more Australian to beat. In one of the great moments of Ashes history, Ettinghausen managed to catch up with a flying Offiah and pushed his foot into touch, denying what would have been a huge start for Britain. Ettinghausen chased him down again a second time later in the match. British skipper Garry Schofield later reflected that the Australian's efforts were the difference between a series win and a loss (they lost). Injury ruled Ettinghausen out of the World Cup final, though – and now, Offiah seemingly had no one to challenge him in the pace stakes.

Finally, twenty years after their last World Cup crown, the Lions had their best chance at toppling Australia. The decision to hold it away from the traditional rugby league grounds – Leeds, Hull or Huddersfield – and use Wembley Stadium, the huge London venue mainly used for soccer, was a big gamble, but showed how popular international rugby league had become. Test footy was back in Britain.

'Here we go, here we go!' Wembley's 73,631 spectators sang in full voice as the Lions and Kangaroos ran out onto the vast field. It certainly wasn't a good night to stay in if you were living in the surrounding streets. The mostly British crowd showed passion never seen at a rugby league Test match in England. Given the heaving atmosphere, New Zealand referee Dennis Hale should have been extremely nervous. Yet when I spoke to him more than twenty years later, he said he took positives from his performance during the Ashes series in Australia a few months earlier.

'The sheer intensity of the occasion was huge – both sides were very strong.' He was 'nervous as hell' during the first Ashes game but had a good match and was invited back for the remaining two Tests. 'I remember thinking: I can do this. It gave me great confidence.'

So, with the man with the whistle ready, the teams braced themselves for what was to be one of the tightest, most absorbing Test matches of the 1990s. Of the players, two of the greatest were skippers – Garry Schofield of Britain and Mal Meninga of Australia. And then there was Martin Offiah. The question still remained: would the Australians be able to catch him?

Simply the best

As Australia and the rest of the world jived to Tina Turner's massive hit *The Best* in 1989, so did the marketing department of the Australian Rugby League. It opened up another advertising masterstroke. They used her and the song to promote the start of the 1990 Winfield Cup season. The lyrics 'simply the best' rang out in the background as she cavorted down Manly beach with Andrew Ettinghausen, Allan Langer and Wayne Pearce, plus danced and partied with a host of other well-known rugby league players during a series of television adverts.

It was a clear message. Rugby league was a game everyone could enjoy. Featuring a mixture of big tackles, Turner in a variety of poses, and players scoring tries and lifting weights, the video appealed to males and females, kids and teenagers. And if you weren't into footy, then you could check out the well sculpted physiques on show too.

The best was about to come: it wasn't the Winfield Cup, but the 1990 Ashes series in Britain. So often in sport, a result can be decided in a split second. All it takes is an error in judgement, a wrong decision taken, or a lapse in concentration. The game is lost or won in the click of a finger. This series was full of such moments.

Ahead of the first Test, Britain's Ashes skipper Ellery Hanley – one of the most talented and versatile players Britain ever produced – was said to have given a speech to his team that falls snugly in the 'reverse psychology' category. It went something like this: 'no one expects you to win, not the fans, not your wives and family, not anyone'. Well, it certainly got the British boys pumped to deliver a rousing statement. And so it was; eighty minutes later Great Britain were 1–0 up, after an adrenaline-thumping 19–12 Test victory in front of a record 54,569 ecstatic fans at Wembley Stadium.

They were all set to reclaim the Ashes in the second match, with the scores level at 10–10 with ten minutes to play. Australian halfback Ricky Stuart had earlier thrown a pass meant for Ettinghausen, but British centre Paul Loughlin stuck out a hand and intercepted it, levelling the scores, but the kick was missed. With less than two minutes left, Stuart made amends. The halfback threw a huge dummy pass, which caused British hooker Lee Jackson to jump out of his line. The Australian five-eighth then ran most of the field before offloading to a rampaging Mal Meninga, who scored the winning try.

Schofield at the time couldn't believe Jackson fell for the dummy, given his status as one of the team's best defenders. He later joked that Jackson should get a job at any baby department store, as they accepted huge dummies too. The Kangaroos ran away with the third Test to keep the Ashes once again.

Meninga's transformation

Leading the Australian team out for the World Cup final seemed a natural fit for man-mountain Mal Meninga. An experienced Test player – he'd made his international debut in 1982 – Meninga had also played a vital role for Queensland and Canberra in series wins and premierships. Yet only five years before the 1992 final, the media thought he was closer to joining a nursing home than playing rugby league. Getting the Australian captaincy was a fanciful notion.

After seven years' setting alight the Brisbane Rugby League competition, in 1984 Meninga accepted a contract with St Helens and scored twenty-eight tries in thirty-one games, helping them to a title and allowing British audiences to see how good he was.

Meninga endured a horror run of injuries between 1987 and 1988, breaking his arm four times. As a result, he missed the World Cup final at Eden Park. The enforced lay-off turned out to be a blessing in disguise as he worked his way back to health by training regularly and pushing his own physical limits. He returned a new, even-better player. After receiving the honour of captaining the Canberra Raiders, he was also rewarded with a return to State of Origin and Test football in 1989, helping Australia to series wins, then the ultimate reward: being named as Australian captain in 1990. There was only one problem. The incumbent Kangaroos captain, Wally Lewis, was recovering from injury and would most likely return to the Australian team in 1991 if deemed fit. Meninga was delighted at receiving the honour but also realistic enough to know it may have been an interim measure.

Lewis recalled a story during his younger years in the Brisbane championship. As fierce rivals, Meninga caught Lewis with an elbow across his face, which he objected to and pointed out his displeasure. Meninga didn't like that – so next time he got the ball, he went looking for Lewis, found him and ran straight over the top of him to score a try. That was the last time Lewis tried to rile the big centre.

Both players were named in the Australian team to take on New Zealand in 1991. The question on everyone's minds was who was going to be selected as captain? The media pestered both players for most of the season. Meninga said he

Their Finest Hour

would happily step aside to make way for the former captain. Lewis just wanted to get his Test spot back. Eventually, Meninga was retained as captain, with Lewis to start at five-eighth.

As it transpired, it made no difference who wore the skipper's armband for the first Test in Melbourne. The young and enthusiastic Kiwis pulled off a stunning 24–8 win against the Kangaroos. It turned out to be Lewis's last game in an Australian jersey. It was a tough night for Australian rugby league and for Lewis himself.

> We got beaten fairly convincingly. I retired from representative football after the match as I felt I didn't have a lot of heart in me at that point; I was a long way off what was needed for Test football. You had to acknowledge the Kiwis and their planning which was very good. Playing for Australia is the greatest honour in the game but family was the most important thing [he found out his daughter was deaf around that time].

With Lewis stepping aside, Meninga was now set to be Australia's captain for the longer term. From a young player with raw talent, 'Big Mal' had become the leader who inspired others by using that talent.

Referee Dennis Hale remembered Meninga as a very straightforward player who was 'a force within himself. If there were any altercations, he would sort them out quickly'. With a team full of some of the world's best players, Meninga was able to bring them all together

168

and inspire by example. During a Test match earlier that year against PNG, Brad Fittler remembers his Australian teammates being low on desire, given the opposition and the location. Yet Meninga, noticing his team's poor attitude and taking umbrage at the lack of pride being shown in representing their country, took it upon himself to take on the tough Papuans and inspired the rest to do the same. That's leadership, and it summed up what Meninga the skipper was all about.

Never fear anyone

On the other side, Great Britain skipper Garry Schofield was a frustrated man. After strongly developing his game at international level in the five-eighth position and orchestrating some great performances, he was moved into the centres for the 1992 World Cup final to accommodate Deryck Fox and Shaun Edwards. Now, on the biggest day in British rugby league since the third Test of the 1990 Ashes series, the creative and cunning Leeds playmaker was stuck in a defensive role. It's something wistful British rugby league fans probably bemoan to this day.

Schofield was the master of the chip and chase. He used it to great effect early in the tackle count when the fullback was deep down the field, which allowed him more chance of regathering possession and eliminated any risk. He'd engineered the play many times in his Test career and given the turgid, bruising nature of the match, a Schofield kick and regather might have changed its stale complexion. Think back to the first Ashes Test in 1990, when the same move inspired the winning try by Paul Eastwood, or in the third Test in 1992, resulting in Martin Offiah crossing over to ensure a big winning margin.

There was no fear either. Schofield's father gave him some sound advice as he rose through the schoolboy ranks and into professional rugby league: 'never fear anyone's reputation'. When he made his international debut against France, then Australia, it was the same story. Marking the likes of Gene Miles and Brett Kenny initially caused some angst; but Schofield senior repeated his mantra, and his son never looked back.

A dizzy debut

Sporting success can sometimes come down to pure timing. Some players ply their trade for years but never manage to reach their potential or play in representative teams. Fullback Tim Brasher wasn't one of these. In one short year, he made such an impression on representative selectors that he was offered a Test debut in the biggest game of all – the World Cup final.

After seeing the teenager play for the Australian Schoolboys team in 1988, Balmain Tigers coach Warren Ryan plucked him out of high school to make his first-grade debut in 1989. Brasher was selected for New South Wales in the final State of Origin match of 1992. As Brasher admits, he 'played half a game', but it was a superb forty minutes, during which he pulled off two try-saving tackles. He continued this success by topping the competition try-scoring charts that year.

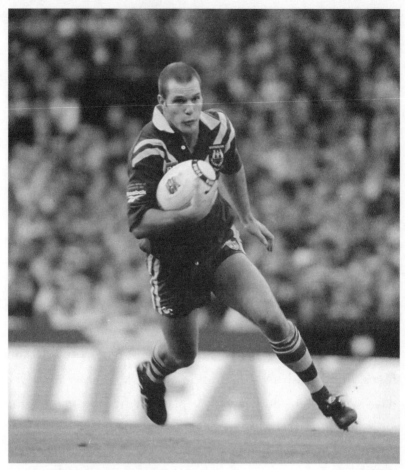

Tim Brasher quickly carved his reputation as Australia's number one fullback in the early to mid-1990s. RLPhotos.com

Brasher didn't have the step or verve of Gary Belcher or the imposing physical presence of Paul Hauff, who both had held the Kangaroos fullback role in previous seasons. But he did have the fearlessness and confidence that great players seem to possess at an early age. He was delighted to tour with the Australian team, and today holds fond memories of the Ashes and Test series as a youngster.

I remember watching events held at Wembley as a kid – FA Cup finals, concerts – and to walk out there in front of the biggest crowd I've played in front of, close to 80,000 people, was amazing. It was a dream that came true – I used to sit up and watch Tests on TV as a kid. I had a warm fuzzy feeling as I walked out.

The Test came around quickly. Brasher's joy turned to horror as early as the first minute. After a strong defensive first set of tackles, the Australians found themselves defending back on their own goal-line after giving away a penalty.

Deryck Fox launched a huge, perfectly placed bomb that zeroed in just outside the Australian try-line. His target: a nervous Brasher. British defenders also narrowed their focus into smashing the rookie fullback. These were the days when you could tackle a player when he was in the air – it was a free-for-all. The forward pack traditionally got most of the plaudits when it came to toughness. But fullbacks and wingers had to endure crushing shoulder-charges and the risk of serious back or neck injuries as they were tackled high off the ground, competing for kicks. Brasher bravely leaped high under the cross bar, but he landed without the ball.

I was seen as a safe fullback who didn't drop kicks. In the final, I dropped a catch in the first five minutes. They kicked a [penalty] goal from the mistake. From there, though, I had one of my best ever games.

As Britain got ahead with a penalty kick through Fox right in front of the posts, Australia still hadn't touched the ball. At the end of the ensuing set – now three sets of six in possession – Lions fullback Joe Lydon was trapped by hooker Steve Walters, who rushed up from dummy half. Lydon slipped as he tried to evade the tackle, and while in the act of slipping a sensational pass to Fox who managed a great kick, the fullback twisted his ankle and had to be replaced later.

The visitors equalled soon afterwards through Meninga's boot to make it 2–2. Fox continued to have a strong game in general player; however, it was his halves partner who could really take it to the Australians: Shaun Edwards.

The little giants

It was fairly easy to track down Edwards. Some ex-players take up relatively normal jobs after their playing days, like former Australian wing Lionel Williamson, who teaches at a school in Queensland. Luckily, I had no dramas finding what Edwards was up to. Now the current Wales rugby union defensive coach, he was happy to have a chat over the phone. The time came and at around eleven in the morning, I thought I might catch him on a quick break from his football duties. He answered in a hushed tone.

'I'm at a pub, mate.' Was he drinking before midday on a Tuesday? I tried to supress my surprise. It came out as giddy laughter. Not the best response. The real reason was far more sombre. 'I'm at a friend's funeral actually,' he said in a low tone. I looked around for the nearest hole to jump into. It wasn't a good start.

Edwards' sporting career has been full of extreme highs – he played for Great Britain thirty-six times and won the Man of Steel award in 1990 – but off the park, he's had his share of personal tragedy. His father, Jack, a professional rugby league player with Warrington, suffered a crippling spinal injury in a match, leaving him unable to work. Later, Edwards contended with his brother dying in a car accident. Yet when he was old enough to hold a rugby ball, his father never discouraged him from playing the sport. Edwards swiftly rose through the ranks as a schoolboy, joining Wigan at eighteen and with them winning eight victories in the Challenge Cup – the most sought-after trophy in British rugby league.

It was a short stint with Balmain in Australia, though, that changed his career. There, he met Michael 'Mickey' Neill, the Tigers' five-eighth.

> Mickey was my inspiration. He had a tremendous never-give-up attitude, never stopped going and had amazing courage. Mickey showed me how much effort I needed to put in to be a consistent player and taught me to always keep learning.

Edwards had a fairly quiet World Cup final. He got sent off after taking out his frustration on an opposition player midway through the second half, although it didn't cost any points for his team. He was ultra-competitive and, despite all the rave reviews, accolades and awards – he won more than thirty medals during his playing career – as it turns out, he only cared about his father's opinion. If his dad was happy with his performance, he was too.

The blond-haired pivot's match-up with pint-sized Queenslander Allan Langer was a wonderful sub-plot as the game wore on. He and Langer, the smallest but most explosive players off the mark, were able to take advantage of the slippery conditions as rain started to come down late in the match. Edwards and Langer were two of their respective country's most celebrated players – Langer continues to coach in the National Rugby League and helps out Queensland's Origin team – and on that afternoon at Wembley, rugby league fans of both nations got to see them at their peak. Tenacious cover tackling by Edwards to stop rampaging Australian runs was priceless for Great Britain, as it left Fox to do most of the general kicking.

Langer had already orchestrated his side's World Cup victory in 1988 with a Man of the Match performance. Now it was his young five-eighth partner who stepped up in his first World Cup performance.

Just blow out your cheekbone

Brad 'Freddy' Fittler wasn't your typical twenty-year-old. Before the age of twenty-one, he'd played six State of Origin matches for New South Wales, won a club premiership with Penrith and made four Test appearances for Australia. His precocious talents were spotted as early as eighteen and he became the youngest man ever selected to go on a Kangaroo tour. By 1992, compared to fellow young guns Tim Brasher and Steve Renouf, Fittler was a grizzled veteran. He was selected in the vital five-eighth role after Laurie Daley was ruled out. Even during his early years, Fittler was relaxed with his football. He was just a young kid having the time of his life, with the best rugby league players in the world.

Crack. Fittler could recall the exact moment British hooker Martin Dermott broke his cheekbone. It was only a few minutes into the final when Fittler stepped off his left foot and braced for the tackle. Denis Betts went low, but Dermott jumped in the air and elbowed him across his cheek. Fittler stayed down, gingerly patting his face. It really hurt.

The young playmaker went to Nathan Gibbs, the team doctor, and got checked out. Gibbs advised it wasn't broken and he could play on. Fittler's right cheek had swelled up like a balloon and was blotchy red. It looked like he'd been hit with a sledgehammer. Whether courageous or naïve, Fittler continued to play the rest of the match. By the end, the right side of his face was as sunken as a collapsed ship. He sought out Gibbs after the match and enquired whether his cheek was actually broken. The doctor replied that if he had told him the truth, he wouldn't have continued playing. I've asked Gibbs for his side of the story, but he declined to comment.

Reilly and Bozo

Meanwhile, in the coaches' boxes, Mal Reilly and Bob Fulton were frantically trying to out-point each other. The last time they were on opposite sides was in the 1970 World Cup final, Reilly as a gritty lock and Fulton as a snappy five-eighth. Now, twenty-two years later – or, the whole lives of Australia's Tim Brasher and Britain's Alan Hunte – they were set to face off in the coaches' boxes for another big trophy, this time as mentors.

Reilly got into rugby league by accident. He played soccer until aged nineteen, but one day upon missing a bus to take him to the game, he joined his mates to play rugby league. It was the last time he played soccer. Reilly went on to do everything possible in the game, winning premierships as both player and coach in Australia and the UK, as well as playing for and coaching his country.

Less than six months after playing for their respective countries in the World Cup, Reilly and Fulton joined up with Manly in the Sydney competition. They helped the Sydney side win premierships in 1972 and 1973.

Reilly's impact on the Australian competition was quite literally instantaneous. According to former Manly forward Peter Peters, ahead of Reilly's debut match against the Rabbitohs, the British forward asked him who the opposition's best player was. The answer: Bob McCarthy. Reilly then instructed Dennis Ward, who kicked off for Manly, to kick the ball out on the full; this meant a scrum would form at halfway. As the touch judges were watching the ball go into touch, Reilly elbowed McCarthy in the head with such force the unsuspecting player was stretchered off and didn't return. In less than sixty seconds he'd played his hand as a hardened, no-nonsense competitor whose will to win was as strong as his gritty forward play.

Although his brand of 'biff and bash' lent itself to several send-offs and a divided reaction among those who saw him play, Reilly's courage was never in doubt: in the '73 grand final, for example, he had six pain-killer injections into his hip. He dished out punishment until he couldn't go on and was replaced. Fulton carried on with Manly, and Reilly returned to England in 1975.

Almost fifteen years later, they returned at the helms of Australia and Britain. Reilly had a good start to his Test coaching career. He says:

> When we went out there in '88 when I first took on
> the GB job, we lost the first two Tests, then came back
> and won the third Test 26–12. All of a sudden, the guys
> took on board a huge dose of confidence and self-belief,
> and we backed it up when Australia came over for the
> following year's tour and we beat them at Wembley. So
> all of a sudden we've got back-to-back successes against
> Australia in Test matches. I was thrilled to be asked to
> coach Great Britain and loved the involvement with the
> players.

He brought steely professionalism and put in place simple game plans that were easily bought into by his players. He reassured his men they were good enough to do well out on the park. Reilly also felt he was able to strengthen his squad's mental toughness and, as a former player himself, could comment on how to meet the high expectations of playing for your country.

'Bozo' Fulton's standing in Australian rugby league was never questioned, given his superb performances during the 1970s. His legacy continued when he was handed the Kangaroos' head coaching role in 1989. He brought a cool head, strong preparation and great man management to his Australians, whom he coached until 1998.

Australian prop Glenn Lazarus spent four years with Fulton's Kangaroos teams from 1990 to 1994. He remembers a great mentor and someone who could keep teams firing well, especially on long tours.

> 'Bozo' was very educated in terms of how to win footy
> games. With the Australian team, he did a very good
> job of bringing a bunch of guys together, especially
> on the Kangaroo tours. That's a tough gig as a coach;
> you've got to keep your team up, players enthused, as
> well as prepare for games every three or four days. He
> did that very well. Usually Tests require at least a week
> of preparation. He was flat out for ten weeks and had
> to keep everyone happy. Bob had a ton of respect from
> everyone for what he achieved in the game.

Lazarus also gave rare insight into what Fulton based his Test game plan around: 'Lucky for me – he had a mantra of "big is beautiful" – and picked the bigger blokes in the squad. I was lucky to be one of the bigger ones so he picked me!'

The Brick with Eyes

Fulton certainly had some large artillery to choose from in the early 1990s. Along with the sizable 1.88 metre, 115 kilogram frame of Lazarus, Paul Sironen was a giant at

1.95 metres at the same weight, with young Paul Harragon, John Cartwright and Mark Sargent adding size and skill to the forward pack. Lazarus went on to become the game's number one prop forward for close to a decade, leading the charge for the Canberra Raiders, Brisbane Broncos, Melbourne Storm, New South Wales and Australia.

After making his first-grade debut in 1987, Lazarus appealed to representative selectors through his impact and strong work ethic. A New South Wales Origin jumper came in 1989, followed by an Australian jersey in the mid-season Test against New Zealand. Lazarus was so proud to represent his country that, when I spoke to him recently, he remembered his place in Australian Test history – Kangaroo number 603. His first tour was a big moment in his career.

> I wish players today could experience it [a Kangaroo tour]. It's an opportunity to room with blokes ten weeks at a time, create long-lasting friendships with guys you wouldn't play against at club level. Players miss out on this nowadays.

It was during his career that tongue-in-cheek radio commentators Roy Slaven and H.G. Nelson called Lazarus 'the brick with eyes'. Lazarus embraced the name and after retiring, used the moniker for his own brand.

Lazarus had to wait until 1992 to play his first Test on home soil. The Australians won 22–6, but it wasn't a personal highlight – he got poleaxed early.

'I don't remember much [of my debut]. Barrie McDermott knocked me out in the first minute when I was on the ground.' Lazarus managed to stay in the game and battled through a heap of defensive work. Operating in today's more safety-conscious environment, he would have been whisked off the park to take a concussion test.

Lazarus played in the next two Tests, enduring a loss and then a win to wrap up a tough Ashes series. Club success with Brisbane followed later that year. When it came to the World Cup match, Lazarus was already a contented man.

> It was a big year for Brisbane [they had eight players
> selected in the Australian squad]. We'd also made finals
> of the Sevens, Grand Final and World Club Challenge
> after the Test match. Great Britain were a tough team –
> much harder again on home ground.

His bulk had immediate impact as he carried three British players on his back with his first carry in the match. For such a big man he also had incredible ball skills. Lazarus had the presence of mind – and the execution – to toe through a grubber kick after Meninga missed a penalty attempt, as well as produce a one-handed pass away in a tackle to give his team the momentum. He wasn't just 'a brick with eyes' after all. Although catchy, the moniker didn't do his talent as a footballer justice.

> It was such an important honour in the game of rugby
> league to play in a World Cup final, and represent your

country on foreign shores. [The performance] was
very satisfying at a time when England were a pretty
good side, very competitive and would fight tooth
and nail. That match was the greatest highlight of my
representative career.

Deryk Fox continued his excellent form with the boot,
landing a forty-two-metre penalty goal with ease. Meninga
then responded with another goal at closer range. It was 4–4.
On the stroke of half-time, referee Ward awarded a penalty
to Britain around twenty metres out, ruling Ben Elias's pass
was deliberately forward. Fox converted to give his team a
6–4 scoreline.

Brasher's last bomb

Tim Brasher continued to work hard in attack after his early
blunder. With the gruelling defensive efforts on show by
both forward packs, the fatiguing affair was slowly allowing
more space for the quicker men to display their wares. The
fullback remained fairly underutilised on defence as the
British game was focused on playing the territory game,
consisting of driving long kicks deep into the Australian half
and then waiting for a mistake. Unfortunately for them, this
Australian team didn't make many mistakes.

Great Britain got a good field position with twenty
minutes to go, around thirty metres out from Australia's
goal posts. Fox stepped up, launching a high kick that
floated in the air. The crowd suddenly rose as one; instead
of thirteen players running towards Brasher and the ball,

it felt like there were now 70,000. Crowds understand the ebb and flow of a game, when the important moments are happening. Fox's kick was Britain's best chance of taking a commanding lead. As the ball was right in the centre of the field, a try would mean a simple conversion in front of the uprights, therefore an eight-point lead, meaning Australia would need to score twice to get ahead. The game hung on this kick.

Brasher saw two British players out of the corner of his eye who were running straight for him. He needed to remain focused on catching the football, though, despite the blue and white wall zeroing in. He, like the crowd, realised how crucial a clean take would be in the game's context.

'I had to take it. I was nervous, but had to do it. If I dropped it, they would probably score.'

As the ball began its descent to Earth, the crowd were generating so much noise that any noise restrictions outside the stadium were shattered. Brasher leapt high in the air. So did British fullback Alan Tait, who'd replaced the injured Joe Lydon. Both players seemed to have the ball as they landed on the ground. Most crucially for Australia, the ball never touched the ground. The result: Hale confirmed the ball was held up and Australia got a tap restart. It was ruled that Brasher caught the ball cleanly in his own goal. The debutant had saved the day. Australia lifted. Britain sagged. Having dodged Britain's huge left hook, the Kangaroos were about to throw their own knockout punch. Enter Kevin Walters.

The Walters boys

Steve, Kevin and Kerrod Walters all dreamt of playing for Australia as they fought out mini-Test matches in their backyard in Ipswich, Queensland.

All talented rugby league players, they steadily rose through the ranks for their clubs, state and finally their country. By 1991, all three had played for Australia. Yet they hadn't played together in the same Australian team. Kerrod replaced Steve (who was suspended) in the 1991 Australian team to play New Zealand in the Trans-Tasman Test series, as both were hookers. Kevin travelled on the 1990 Kangaroo Tour to Great Britain and France but had to wait until the next year to play a match.

1992 was a watershed year of huge proportions for the Walters family. Twins Kerrod and Kevin combined to help Brisbane win that year's club premiership, while eldest brother Steve played a big part in Australia's Ashes series win. So, on the plane back after celebrating the Brisbane Broncos' premiership victory in 1992, one punter asked the boys' mum whether all three would be picked in the Australian squad to contest the World Cup final – a not altogether far-fetched suggestion. She advised the supporter, 'They would be if I was a selector.' As it turns out, perhaps the selection staff consulted Sandy Walters after all, because they were all named later that night.

Steve and Kevin were selected in the final seventeen, with Kerrod missing out to his elder brother, who took the hooker's position. Kevin remembers he needed to do something special once he got on the park. Bradley Clyde got injured shortly after half-time and it was at this point that coach Fulton gave notice to Kevin he would be on soon.

He noticed the British lacked numbers near the touch-line. Kevin looked at Steve Renouf and that quick eye contact was enough to start the move. Walters flung a long pass out to Renouf, who accelerated through the space, running twenty metres to score a try that came from nowhere. The British were shell-shocked. What had just happened?

Shaun Edwards called it a 'play straight out of the Broncos coaching manual' and was the 'one mistake' that cost his team the World Cup. In sport, that's all that can be required to change a match. Meninga converted the side-line goal and suddenly Australia had a 10–6 lead.

The Pearl shines

The 'outball'. It sounds like a baseball term. But this is the move that Edwards was referring to, as Wayne Bennett's Brisbane team had perfected it during their march to the premiership that year. Allan Langer, Kevin Walters and Steve Renouf were the key exponents. Langer would give it to Walters, who timed his run and fired a long pass to Renouf. The objective was to get the centre, and the ball, on the outside of the opposition defender, who was stuck flat-footed, watching the player. The trio had practised it in Broncos training, then in games, throughout the whole of 1992.

So when the three were called up to play for Australia for the first time as a group, this very effective play was about to be unleashed in front of a disbelieving Wembley crowd. It was a stunning try and Renouf hardly got a touch on him, like many other times that season. Blink once and the try was scored. British centre John Devereux had no chance.

The 'outball' and other club inventions were not divulged at Kangaroo training sessions, though. When the trio played for Australia again, their teammates would naturally want to know how they went about forming the move. Walters made his younger teammate keep quiet – not wanting to spill the 'Broncos' secrets'. It is amazing to think that the Australian rugby league team could have been even better if they'd shared their philosophies and plays that worked so well at club level. Even in the early 1990s, there was still a divide along team loyalties. It is both shocking and disappointing in equal measure. Perhaps they were still yet to embrace the professionalisation of the game in its entirety.

If there were any doubts about the young Renouf's ability to perform on the big stage, his brilliant solo try in the 1992 grand final pushed those firmly to one side. It came after an eighty-metre run that showcased his pace and determination, giving the Broncos an insurmountable lead.

With great professional success came personal happiness too. Only weeks later, Renouf's partner Lis gave birth to their first child, a baby boy called Samuel Bruce. Earlier that year, he'd had to come to terms with his father's death at just sixty-two. Renouf's life had changed from developing footballer to Australian representative and Queensland celebrity, young father and media personality. Steve Renouf would be a mainstay of the Queensland and Australian teams for the next seven years.

His rise to rugby league greatness began in the small Queensland town of Murgon. He was one of ten children, all of whom were very talented in sport. All young Steve wanted to do was run with the football. Rugby league became an instinctive, wonderful pursuit. Renouf was hooked. The way he glided across the field is very similar to Christian Cullen, the rugby union fullback who arrived on the scene a few years later. Both players had a style that was all their own.

Deep into the final ten minutes of the final, the teams' intensity levels were dropping. It was a bruising, energy-sapping match. It wasn't a great rugby league spectacle. Martin Offiah couldn't get into the game despite the massive pre-match hype.

Great Britain was able to conjure up one final shot. With a penalty and possession now ten metres from the Australian try-line, the rain started falling heavily. Schofield threw a long pass for his winger, but Meninga stuck out a hand, knocking it down and stopping the momentum. Another scrum, a penalty, and big British forward Andy Platt, who was strong all day, thundered into the defensive line. He tried to get a pass away with full-time only seconds away, but it slipped forward in his attempt. The hooter sounded, referee Hale blew his whistle. Australia had hung on. There were no wild celebrations. It was just pure relief.

Britain bemoaned the one that got away. It was their best chance since the 1970 World Cup, but they couldn't find something extra to breach the Australians' defence.

After the match, skipper Schofield admitted to *Rugby League Week* that Britain's game plan changed for the worse in the selection of Fox at halfback. Fox, although possessing a booming boot, was more of a defensive, tactical player on a day when they needed to try and unlock the Australian defence through creativity.

It wasn't all gloomy for Great Britain. Their strong performances against both Australia and New Zealand meant that international rugby league administrators could look forward to consistently big crowds. Another Ashes series beckoned in 1994, with the centenary of rugby league World Cup to be held in 1995. Club football in Australia and England was in good health, crowds were flocking to the grounds and players were reaping the benefits too. Yet rugby league was about to be rocked, split up and divided. The Super League war was around the corner.

Scoreboard: **Australia 10** (Steve Renouf try; Mal Meninga 3 goals) defeated **Great Britain 6** (Deryck Fox 3 goals). Crowd: 73,631.

Match 7, 1995

JUST PRAY IT MISSES

Australia v. New Zealand

Alfred McAlpine Stadium, Huddersfield, England
22 October 1995
World Cup semi-final

AUSTRALIA	NEW ZEALAND
1. Tim Brasher	1. Matthew Ridge (captain)
2. Rod Wishart	2. Sean Hoppe
3. Mark Coyne	3. Kevin Iro
4. Terry Hill	4. Richie Blackmore
5. Brett Dallas	5. Richie Barnett
6. Brad Fittler (captain)	6. Tony Kemp
7. Geoff Toovey	7. Stacey Jones
8. Dean Pay	8. John Lomax
9. Andrew Johns	9. Henry Paul
10. Mark Carroll	10. Jason Lowrie
11. Steve Menzies	11. Stephen Kearney
12. Gary Larson	12. Quentin Pongia
13. Jim Dymock	13. Mark Horo
Interchange:	Interchange:
14. Robbie O'Davis	14. Gene Ngamu
15. Matthew Johns	15. Hitro Okesene
16. Jason Smith	16. Ruben Wiki
17. Nik Kosef	17. Tony Iro
Coach: Bob Fulton	Coach: Frank Endacott

Referee: Russell Smith

As a rugby league coach for the Kiwis, Frank Endacott focused on man management. He aimed to create an environment of cohesiveness and good team spirit instead of focusing too much on the technical side of the game. His job was to bring his teams closer together and by his reckoning if his players were happy, then he believed they would perform better. The UK rugby league media nicknamed him 'Happy Frank', based on his perennially positive disposition and ability to take criticism well, no matter how scathing it was. Endacott's press conferences never had any vitriol or hatred after a loss. It never cost anyone to give a smile – this was his day-to-day motto.

Don't let the smiling impression fool you, though. Endacott didn't take any rubbish from any of his players – or anyone else for that matter – and summed up opposition teams in a thorough way. Before the 1995 World Cup semi-final against Australia, he wrote down the names of his Kiwi team on a chalkboard and then proceeded to rattle off why he wouldn't swap his players for anyone – least of all the Australians. Yet he summed up the challenge he was faced that night with this thought:

'As coach, I was told if you can win one game against Australia, you are doing OK.'

Endacott's predecessors would sympathise with that statement. Tony Gordon had managed only one win in five attempts against Australia. Bob Bailey achieved a victory in four matches but ended his tenure with 0–44 and 12–40 drubbings. Howie Tamati, who Endacott replaced, managed a draw and two losses when facing the Kangaroos. Even the celebrated Graham Lowe, who is regarded as one of the Kiwis' most successful coaches, could only produce a brace of wins in eight matches during the mid-1980s. It is only in the modern era that a coach, Stephen Kearney, has had a string of consistent results against the Australians.

New Zealand had prepared well leading into the 1995 World Cup. NZRL chairman Ray Haffenden arranged the New Zealand squad to spend some time with the Special Air Service, an elite and highly specialised combat unit of the country's Defence Force. He felt it would be good to put the players through hardship and bring them all to the same level. 'They were about to head to a fairly combative environment in England, so this experience would make them tougher and build team spirit,' he says.

Endacott was confident of his side's capabilities after winning both pool matches. Also, Australia looked relatively beatable after their first-up loss against England, their first defeat in ten World Cup fixtures going back to 1988. Endacott sat down and planned his training schedule with a clear mind and positive thoughts.

Yet the week beginning 14 October 1995 would represent the worst time in Frank Endacott's coaching career. The events of that Tuesday and Wednesday had nothing to do with injuries, game plans or skills drills. Led by captain Matthew Ridge, the players argued with the New Zealand Rugby League over payments that were promised earlier that year but for reasons unknown never eventuated, or else there was a breakdown in communication between parties.

Money and greed were at the core of the sport's problems between 1995 and 1997 after Rupert Murdoch and News Limited created a new, expansionist and cashed-up 'Super League', shaking up rugby league's traditional values and promising wild injections of cash. NZRL chief executive Graham Carden had signed with Super League earlier in the year. Now, at the worst possible time for everyone in the Kiwi camp, those grievances were aired.

The feeling within the New Zealand playing group, mainly from the more experienced players like Ridge and Richie Blackmore, was that they weren't getting fair compensation to play for their country. Ridge later let his frustrations out in his autobiography. Blackmore was particularly forthright when he recalled his take on events.

> Playing for your country was the highest honour
> you could achieve in your sport; it didn't get much
> bigger than playing Australia either. Our frustrations
> stripped down to the basic idea of being valued by your
> organisation and getting compensated for that high
> performance. How could you expect to play for the
> Kiwis but given a pittance in return?

Thankfully, an agreement was reached – much to the relief of Endacott and the rest of the coaching and management team. The squad pulled together quickly after that and focused on their preparation. Yet in rugby league's time of discontent, dollar signs were in everyone's eyes. How far could relationships be tested?

Cash is king

Maurice Lindsay was a happy man. In April 1995, executives from News Limited put to him an audacious vision of a global expansion of rugby league. Lindsay was the chairman of the Rugby Football League and the International Rugby League Board. In his view, the promises of instant cash and a new image came at the best possible time.

Honest, unflinching and articulate, Lindsay had watched with sadness as rugby league in England fell to tragic lows in the late 1970s and 1980s. An image of pot-bellied, sluggish players who were brawlers rather than ball-players led the domestic scene to flop to its lowest point when Wigan was relegated to the second division in 1979. Wigan had a proud league history and for long had represented success in the sport; now they were all but extinct. As a result, television largely stayed away from broadcasting the English competition, with only fleeting coverage. Crowds stayed away from watching live matches too. Rugby league in England, it seemed, was about to go the way of the dinosaurs.

So, when News Limited proposed a competition that would give English rugby league a massive injection of money, investment and sponsorship, Lindsay was very thankful. He negotiated a deal worth £87 million over five years and overnight it changed everything. The spin-off was immense. The English game was rescued financially as investors came flooding in. New stadiums were built, regional and local authorities invested, new club ownership and players – the game lifted off.

Australian Rugby League chairman Ken Arthurson was furious. News Limited had emerged from the shadows with a bag of cash to entice his stable of players, together with a plan to destroy the Australian Rugby League and create a new competition.

Passionate, genuine and considered in his approach, Arthurson had watched in delight as rugby league in Australia had thrived ever since Tina Turner had spruiked her songs alongside the Winfield Cup's image years before. State of Origin was booming. The Kangaroos had just retained the Ashes in England. Commercially, the ARL had plenty of sponsors, money and excellent media coverage through television and radio. He'd welcomed four new teams to the competition – two from Brisbane, plus one each from Adelaide and Auckland – to make it twenty teams for an exciting 1995 season.

Whispers of a rebel competition had been raised as early as late 1993, and the rumours continued the following year. Arthurson had maintained the view that if someone wanted to create a new competition, that was fine; as long as the ARL governed it and ran the show, then no problems.

From the first day in April 1995 Super League scouts made their move in what was essentially corporate darkness. Players were taken into hotel rooms at all hours of the day and offered extremely generous contract upgrades. Snatch-and-grab experts would have been impressed. There was certainly a military precision about how the operation was reportedly conducted.

While the fight for rugby league's future in Australia was waging, in England Maurice Lindsay had absolute clarity of thought on one project that was extremely close to his heart: the World Cup.

A proper World Cup

In late 1994, Lindsay went to the International Rugby League Board meeting with a series of documents that would set the future of international rugby league in motion. He had plans for a different World Cup tournament the following year. Lindsay felt embarrassed by the most recent competition offerings: they were drawn out over years and confused the public. Although the final match between Great Britain and Australia in 1992 was a great game, it was only the last in a cycle of matches. Lindsay looked across to what rugby union had done, having staged genuine World Cups in 1987 and 1991.

> The rest of the sporting world used to laugh at us. World Cup? What World Cup? Rugby union was going through a little bit of disarray themselves and only went professional in 1995. They saw us running a novel ten-nation World Cup. It was almost as if they were saying, 'The rugby league boys are in the room now, let's watch them and see how they go.' We were on trial to the sporting world.

Lindsay's vision was to include an expanded competition consisting of some emerging nations. For the first time, the Pacific islands were represented – by Tonga, Samoa, Fiji and

Papua New Guinea. South Africa came in for the first time; Great Britain was broken up into England and Wales; while Australia, New Zealand and France took their usual places. His report was a comprehensive analysis of everything, including budgets, playing grounds and implementation.

The Rugby Football League boss was supremely confident he could get the job done given the right tools. Firstly he had to convince his Australian counterpart, Ken Arthurson, to get on board. To his credit, Lindsay says, Arthurson was very supportive. Although a United Kingdom representative was chairman of the International Board, Australia carried huge influence. Australia had a history of showing only lukewarm interest in international rugby league at that point. Lindsay was delighted when Arthurson was so receptive to his new ideas.

> The truth was that although Australia are the leaders of our game, and they have been tremendous help in terms of spreading rugby league throughout the world, no one there thought outside the box. They were so caught up in their own premiership competition and State of Origin that the World Cup meant nothing to them. [Australian] Wayne Bennett was one big supporter, though; he was a true international expansionist. Ken Arthurson could have easily pulled the plug on it. But to his credit he backed me on the idea.

'An omelette you couldn't unscramble'

Depending on where you stood, Rupert Murdoch was either a true visionary or a corporate mercenary. He'd probably never watched a game of rugby league in his life. Yet he saw the potential of pay television as early as the 1980s and, in Australia, sport and rugby league were just waiting to be tapped into. Put on a service where you could watch football as often as you wanted and it would be a goldmine. Cricket and rugby league were the two most high-profile sports in Australia in the 1990s. Murdoch decided to go after the thirteen-man code.

Former Kangaroo and Queensland representative John Ribot became the key man in these plans. As a member of the Australian 'Invincibles' in 1982, he'd seen how popular rugby league could be internationally and as a marketable product. He took on the CEO role of the new Brisbane Broncos team in 1988 and quickly showed a healthy passion for expanding the game and pushing the traditional boundaries of running a sporting club. The Broncos were a huge commercial success and differentiated themselves from all the other clubs through their marketing. The organisation was out to make a profit first and foremost. Ribot made sure that the people of Brisbane were talking about their rugby league team throughout the winter, whether it was the appointment of Wally Lewis as inaugural captain or the spruiking of their sponsors' products and logos after matches. These edgy tactics didn't sit well with the New South Wales Rugby League, which wanted all NSW clubs to fall in line by having the same approach to merchandising and branding. Ribot wanted his club to be the best and most successful.

Tensions boiled over in 1993, when Ribot proposed that the Winfield Cup grand final be staged in Brisbane, rather than Sydney. But the idea was rejected. Ribot was getting sick of the NSWRL's inward-thinking mindset. When a chance meeting between Brisbane Broncos and News Limited executives occurred in 1993, the seeds of a partnership were sown. Ribot decided to take his chance and was made Chief Executive Officer of the new 'Super League' organisation in 1995, therefore directly competing against his former governing body.

What was News Limited's pitch?

Rugby league would become a truly global, full-time sport. It would be united across Australia, Britain, New Zealand, France and the Pacific island nations, with only the code's best talent playing. With a seemingly infinite supply of money at their disposal, Super League would also look after players' welfare, including insurance, a bigger slice of merchandise revenue and career opportunities after retirement. It looked like a forward-thinking plan that appealed to players and clubs. In return, News would buy the pay TV rights worldwide.

The ARL was blind to what was about to happen. It was during the first two weeks of April 1995 that the Super League executives made their move.

Lightning speed was the order of the day. Players, coaches and eventually clubs were signed quickly. But through the haze of deals and handshakes, a nineteen-year-old prop from the Parramatta Eels called Adam Ritson changed things dramatically by refusing to sign anything without consulting his manager Steve Gillis. I spoke to Gillis about his recollection of this time. As a brand new player agent right in the middle of this stormy time, he branded these moments as 'an omelette you couldn't unscramble'. It certainly was a big mess.

Ritson eventually decided on staying with the Australian Rugby League. Up until this point, seemingly every other player had signed without question. Ritson's gutsy decision halted some of Super League's momentum.

Overseas, the England and New Zealand boards signed with the rebel organisation shortly afterwards. Suddenly, the ARL was a lame duck, isolated from the rest of the rugby league world and completely on its own.

The international season carried on, yet Australia's squad was weakened as the ARL refused to pick Super League-aligned players for international games. The likes of Laurie Daley, Ricky Stuart, Andrew Ettinghausen, Glenn Lazarus and Steve Renouf weren't in contention. Even so, Australia still dispatched New Zealand 3–0 in their mid-season Test series. The Australians were under siege, but they still prospered with their fresh-faced squad.

All the while, in the UK Lindsay continued to plan his tour de force at the end of the year. He needed to create a blockbuster; luckily he struck gold with an idea.

The ultimate diva

In the mid-1990s, Diana Ross was the go-to girl for performing at world events. She opened the soccer World Cup in 1994 and continued to be a bankable star through her big-hearted performances, even though the height of her popularity was probably twenty-five years in the past.

Attracting a superstar like Ross meant that rugby league was serious about staging a proper event. It would give massive credibility.

Much to Lindsay's delight, she said yes, she would love to sing at the Rugby League World Cup. There were a few conditions, though, that only a real pop star would make. Lindsay takes up the story.

> Firstly, Diana insisted on flying via Concorde both ways. She was to be picked up in the airport in either a Rolls Royce or a Bentley and stay at the Dorchester or at least a similar hotel. Her fee was to be 100,000 US dollars. I said yes to it all. But it was really worth it. We marketed it well – [England halfback] Shaun Edwards agreed to take part in a promotion with Diana as a 'Beauty and the Beast' campaign. It got fantastic publicity in the national press. I got in trouble afterwards for spending all that money, though, when the Super League nastiness set in. The Australians objected to her appointment – but it brought a world status to the event. They thought all that spending was unnecessary. But they were wrong.

With Ross's signature secured, the rugby league fireworks were about to get underway. A patient England team lived up to the media's pre-tournament predictions and managed a 20–16 win against Australia. New Zealand squared off against Tonga, a tricky opponent with a few aces in their pack. By the game's end, Lindsay's gamble to create a bigger tournament would be mightily justified.

Duane and Goliath

To illustrate Mike McClennan's passion for rugby league, you need to go back to one Saturday afternoon in the late 1980s in Auckland. He was coaching the senior Mt Albert side, which played in the city's domestic competition. As he took his players into the dressing room and opened the door, out gushed an ocean of water. Those young upstarts who played earlier in the day had left the changing rooms in a watery mess. A furious McClennan decided to take quick action. He stormed upstairs to the boardroom of Auckland Rugby League's headquarters. There, he helped himself to the room's carpet, angrily ripping squares of it up, enough to cover the changing room floor. No team of his would have to sit in a room with their boots soaking wet.

McClennan's players always came first, whether they were juniors, senior club or international teams. It was this single-mindedness – and intensity – that made him the perfect coach to bring out the passion and skill of the new Tongan side.

McClennan only got into coaching when his son Brian started playing. He coached Mt Albert, winning four grand finals in the 1980s, then had successful stints in England with St Helens and Wigan.

McClennan had been around underdog teams for many years: Mt Albert and Northcote weren't favoured to win their competitions. Tonga were 250–1 outsiders going into their first World Cup. So what was his secret in moulding teams together so quickly?

I place punctuality and attendance as very important.
The Tongan boys were amazing – all of them. Even
things like helping old ladies with their bags, acting
properly around others was really good. The manager
of the hotel we stayed in told me they were the best
behaved of any team he'd ever seen.

In front of a small but vocal crowd of just over 8,000 at
England's Warrington Stadium, New Zealand got ready
to play Tonga for the first time. Tonga had a trump card
up their sleeve besides McClennan, though: Duane Mann,
the former Kiwi (twenty-nine Tests between 1989 and
1994), who was deemed surplus to New Zealand's World
Cup squad in 1995. Mann had played more than a hundred
games for Warrington in the past few years and had a good
knowledge of English conditions. Frank Endacott still shakes
his head in sadness when recalling the circumstances that led
to his axing from the Kiwis.

I pencilled in Duane as my hooker and captain for the
World Cup before I went into the selection meeting.
There were three selectors involved at that time. By
the end of it, Duane wasn't even in the team, let alone
being the captain. I remember telling him after that
meeting and it gives me shivers even today when I
think about it. Duane was a really decent man and
a great player. From that moment on, I made sure I
was the sole selector so that type of incident couldn't
happen again.

Tonga in effect gained three players with Mann: captain, hooker and general-play kicker. McClennan was delighted with his new addition.

'Duane was very, very good, a standout operator,' McClennan remembered. 'He had a strong technical understanding of the game. Duane knew Warrington Stadium well – he had played for them over the last three to five years – and knew every blade of grass by first name.' Along with Mann, Solomon Haumono, Angelo Dymock and George Mann, the Tongans weren't short of pluck or inspiration.

McClennan felt Kiwis fullback Matthew Ridge's tendency to stand close to his teammates in defence rather than drop back in anticipation for a long kick was a weakness. So, skipper Mann kicked early in the Tongan's tackle count, causing the New Zealanders to fatigue quicker by turning and chasing. The Tongans would then work hard in defence, giving the opposition halves pairing little time or space to move. The tactic started to pay off in a big way.

Led by Duane Mann, Tonga managed to score a number of tries in the second half and the Kiwis looked sloppy when replying. New Zealand needed thirteen points in ten minutes to win. Centre Richie Blackmore later recalled feeling truly terrified at the prospect of losing and questioned whether he and his Kiwi teammates would be let back into New Zealand, such was the potential backlash if they lost that night.

New Zealand suddenly woke up. It was as if someone slapped a huge fish across the face of every player in a black jersey at once. The Kiwis got possession back and managed a sweeping back-line move, finishing with replacement Hitro Okesene crashing over for a try in the corner. Ridge's quick but accurate conversion made it 18–24. There were six minutes left. What happened next is shrouded in controversy but still makes for a good story.

Tonga ended up with a scrum in their own half. It was at this point that McClennan put the call out to his team to slow the game down. Angelo Dymock stayed down after a tackle for a few minutes. This was supposed to frustrate the opposition and make them more likely to make a mistake. As Dymock was getting helped back to his feet, referee David Campbell seemingly lost count of how many tackles Tonga had left. Instead of their full five tackles, at the third tackle there was a clear call of 'last tackle'.

Frank Endacott swears that it was one of his own players who said it. Whatever happened, Tonga kicked from the next play and therefore missed out on another two tackles, as well as giving New Zealand a better field position to attack from. From the ensuring set, Henry Paul managed a nice offload, with Sean Hoppe, Kevin Iro and finally Richie Blackmore finishing the movement for a try. Ridge converted and the scores were now tied at 24-all with a minute to play. The captain then calmly potted over a drop goal to get the Kiwis a 25–24 victory. Tony Iro shook his head in equal parts disbelief and relief.

That night, the Tongans hosted a massive party with supporters and players from both teams in celebration for what was one of the great matches, but also for a game symbolising a real World Cup at long last.

A Welsh revival

When Maurice Lindsay split up the Great Britain side into England and Wales, the casual observer would have guessed that England wouldn't lack for player numbers. But Wales? Rugby union is their national sport. They don't have a league team, right? The Welsh rugby league team does have a proud history – they stood tall in the 1975 and 1977 World Cups – but since then, the national team had largely been in hibernation. In 1991, Lindsay called the one man who could awaken it from its slumber: Clive Griffiths. He and his Welsh side's incredible performances during this World Cup would unite the whole of Wales for those few weeks.

A dual Welsh rugby union and league international, Griffiths appreciated the start rugby union gave to his sporting career, but really savoured his transfer to rugby league and its lasting impact on his life. Rugby league was a professional game even back in the 1970s. Griffiths signed up to play for St Helens. It changed his life, setting himself up financially as well as providing well for his family. He did a coaching course while still playing, got a spot with Warrington and, in 1991, received a call from Lindsay asking him to coach Wales. It was a quick 'yes' and straight to work.

The coach's first point of business was to appoint a skipper. He had no hesitation in selecting Jonathan Davies, a dual rugby union and league player. Davies was a household name in both codes and a proud Welshman to boot. Next, Griffiths needed to create a team. He was lucky:

Clive Griffiths masterminded Wales' amazing 1995 and 2000 World Cup runs. He and his two sons Owain and Rhys all played for Wales, with Owain (left) Wales' 500th international. Clive Griffiths

We had a mixture of high-profile real rugby league players like David Young, John Devereux, Scott Gibbs, Paul Moriarty, Kelvin Skerrett, Iestyn Harris, as well as some rugby union converts. Everyone came together and bonded really well which helped get them through difficult moments. It was a club team at international level with the closeness and camaraderie. I never had any problem getting them fired up before a game.

Wales' first match of the World Cup was against France in Cardiff. Attracted by the prospect of watching a host of ex-rugby union and league stars, a huge crowd turned up to the stadium. The Welsh public had watched their beloved rugby union team bow out of the other code's World Cup in

June, only winning against Japan. Wales needed something to cheer about.

The local boys started well, with Paul Moriarty showing off his great passing skills and winger Anthony Sullivan scoring a hat trick. Wales led 14–0 at half-time and, despite a late French try, the Welsh had started with a win.

Former All Blacks winger Va'aiga Tuigamala and his enthusiastic Western Samoan team lay in wait for the Welsh in their last pool match. It would determine who made the semi-finals. Davies' son also appreciated the giant-sized task ahead of the more diminutive Welsh players while performing his duties as team mascot on the field. Overawed at the huge frames of the Pacific islanders, young Sam pulled on his dad's shirt and said, 'Wow Dad, they are so big aren't they!' 'Quiet!' said his father. It was true: the imposing Samoans had demolished France to the tune of 56–10 earlier in the week, their physical power laying the foundation for ten tries.

Griffiths' men racked up early points again, with Sullivan and Iestyn Harris grabbing a try each. After two further drop goals by Davies and Harris, the crowd started to sing the national anthem as if they knew victory was almost theirs. Then, halfback Kevin Ellis scooted over to score the winning try. The crowd erupted in an outpouring of joy. Harris gave an insight into what it meant to play for Wales after the match, when he said the crowd were worth at least another ten points for them. The Western Samoans showed how much potential the island nations had with their excellent performances in the Cup. Tonga also did well.

Incredibly, Wales had reached the World Cup semi-final. At least 10,000 fans travelled from Wales to watch their team take on England at the mighty Old Trafford at Manchester. Given the huge interest, more than 2,000 other fans were unable to get into the packed stadium. The English sprinted away in the second half despite only leading 7–4 at one stage, and the dream was over for the gallant Welsh. They were a proud nation that night despite the result.

With England through to the World Cup final, Australia and New Zealand would clash in the other semi-final. It would rate as one of the great games in rugby league history.

An inspired start

Alfred McAlpine Stadium in Huddersfield was silent as New Zealand and Australia walked out onto the pitch. In complete contrast to the heaving, excitable display by the crowd in England's pool match against Australia, the mood at the semi-final was initially subdued – it may have been tension or nerves. The Kiwis had an unexpected supporter base in the stands that day: English fans. It wasn't simply because of the Kiwis' underdog status. They had a vested interest in seeing New Zealand win. England's preference was surely to play the men in black rather than those in green-and-gold.

Both coaches played some tricks with their line-ups before kick-off. Bob Fulton named Andrew Johns at hooker despite the twenty-year-old being a halfback, with Geoff Toovey controlling play from the number seven jersey. Johns would move into first receiver during attacking phases, a decision designed to bring his long passing game into play.

Counting Brad Fittler at five-eighth as well, Australia had three genuine attacking options either side of the ruck. The Kiwis could use Matthew Ridge or a young Stacey Jones, with Endacott putting in live-wire utility Henry Paul at hooker. As Endacott would later say, Paul didn't know what he was going to do next, so how would the Kangaroos? With the chess pieces shuffled, the match got underway on an overcast Huddersfield afternoon.

The Kiwis still firmly believed they had the squad to defeat the Kangaroos, but early on in the match that notion would be in doubt, and Endacott would be sweating slightly under his charcoal black suit. Australia seemingly picked up where they left off during the mid-season Test series, scoring two tries and showing how potent the Toovey–Johns–Fittler attacking axis could be.

Australia struck first in the fourth minute. Tim Brasher was the benefactor of Johns' bullet pass to Fittler, who turned the ball inside to the fullback who scored the first try. The second try caused the Kiwis' heads to drop. Johns again was the supplier, controlling a wayward pass that bounced in front of him. With an outrageous skilfulness that demonstrated his brilliance, he batted the ball to Steve Menzies with the back of his hand. The second-rower held on and dived over to score. Richie Blackmore remembered having that sinking feeling about now:

In the early 1990s, for New Zealand to have any hope of beating the Aussies, we needed our players not only to play at a higher level than we would normally, but also the Australians to play terribly. If that wasn't improbable enough, we also required an element of luck to go our way, maybe the bounce of the ball. When Johns displayed that fortuitous piece of brilliance and Menzies scored, our heads went down. Oh no! Here we go again!

Ridge landed a couple of penalty goals to bring his side back into the match, but Mark Coyne's evasive run right on half-time meant the Kiwis were still chasing the game. The Kangaroos led 14–4 at the break. If there was anything the Kiwis could hold on to it was that Johns had kicked one goal from four attempts, whereas Ridge had a perfect record. The crowd was about to witness one of the greatest tries by a forward in rugby league a few minutes into the second half.

Menzies announces himself on the big stage

Five tries in the World Cup, twenty-two tries for Manly during the club season. It was certainly a big year for the man known as 'Beaver'. Menzies was very different to other forwards of his era. He represented the first incarnation of a forward who could score tries as fast as any member of the back-line. He had enough pace to outflank most wingers and fullbacks, strong awareness and a good step. In his book, *Beaver: The Steve Menzies Story*, he described himself as instinctive, reactive and natural on the football field. By playing the game in front of him, he could take opportunities when they presented themselves.

So when Johns and Fittler combined to give Menzies a hint of an opportunity in the forty-eighth minute, Menzies made the best of it. Sensing a gap opening up, the young forward burst through and sped past Stacey Jones, gliding past halfway like a tearaway racehorse. Sean Hoppe, the fastest man in the New Zealand side, caught up with the Australian, but Menzies still had the presence of mind to fend off the flying winger in time to score his second try of the match. Television commentator Ray Warren memorably described the moment: 'Everyone including the police were chasing him but he still scored!'

Australia's ten-point lead had now moved to a match-winning fourteen-point lead. The Kiwis had to score at least three tries or rely on Matthew Ridge's accurate goal kicking to get close. Time was swiftly elapsing. It was shaping up to be another late point-scoring spree by an Australian team against a New Zealand side. These Kiwis were made of sterner material, though. As Johns piloted through the easy conversion, Ridge barked out his instructions. Step it up or go home.

Ridge's left boot

They stepped it up. The Kiwis stopped watching the Australians and started running with intensity in both attack and defence. Henry Paul got involved more; Gene Ngamu ignited his team with some clever switches of play. Stacey Jones ensured quick movement of the football. New Zealand started to play like they really meant it, like a team who believed in themselves.

In a crucial call, referee Russell Smith sin-binned Kangaroo centre Terry Hill after he interfered with Gene

Ngamu's kick restart and play of the ball, so Australia had to play the final seven minutes with only twelve men. If there was ever a villain that fans loved to hate, it was Hill. He sledged like he was making a shoulder-charge. The Kiwis pushed on the accelerator.

Ngamu's big switch of play led to Richie Barnett grabbing a try in the corner. Tony Iro stretched out and scored a quick try, which was quickly followed by a thundering run down the right-hand touchline by his brother Kevin, who crashed over to score also. The crowd finally had found their voice. The scores were tied at 20-all with thirty seconds left. With the conversion from the side-line, Captain Ridge had the chance to put the Kiwis into the World Cup final and knock the Kangaroos out.

Like many of the Australians, Tim Brasher was very nervous as the Kiwis skipper lined up the kick. 'Ridgey is pretty good with the boot. I remember Joey [Andrew] Johns

Terry Hill scoring the winning try in extra time, putting Australia in the World Cup final which they won 16–8 against England. Rugby League Journal

saying behind the post as we gathered in a group, "Now everyone, pray!'"

Ridge lined it up on the right corner, certainly the less-favoured angle for a right-foot kicker. He had struck them well all tournament and during that year's Winfield Cup had an 82 per cent success rate. But something different entered his head on this occasion.

Instead of stroking the ball and playing on the wind, which was blowing differently that day, he decided to hit it hard and low. Like any amateur golfer, sometimes there is a temptation to lift your head too early instead of keeping it down. Well, that is what happened. Ridge topped it. You'd never see Ridge kick like that before or wouldn't again afterwards.

Sport can often be decided in single moments or inches. A coat of paint was the difference in this match.

After getting past halfway with the last set of normal time, Ridge lined up a drop goal attempt. As Brad Fittler ran ahead to prevent it, Ridge was forced onto his left foot. Unlike in the match against Tonga, this attempt was forty-two metres out. He managed to strike it perfectly.

Everything happened in slow motion. Ridge, Fittler, the referee, the crowd: everyone held their breath as the ball turned through the air. It looked right on target. Brasher was in the best position to judge what happened next.

'I was standing straight under the post as he kicked it. It went over my head and went straight past me. I turned around and saw it shave the left upright. Oh man it was so close.' Television replays weren't that conclusive on first viewing either.

Sadly for the Kiwis, Richie Blackmore felt it scuppered any hopes of the Kiwis winning.

> The match was so sapping both psychologically and physically. I think we put so much hope on that going over that when it was ruled not to have, we were in denial about it. We wanted to believe that the officials got the call wrong.

Referee Russell Smith blew for full-time. This would go into extra time like the 1972 World Cup final. With Hill returning from his ten-minute sin-bin, he scored a crucial try early in the first half of extra time. Fittler outstepped Stephen Kearney and Ridge to put an exclamation mark on the victory. Australia hung on to win 30–20.

The best of the rest

Australia went on to defeat England in the final 16–8 in what coach Bob Fulton rated as the pinnacle of his illustrious coaching career. The British press had made it clear to him how lowly they rated his team going in; the coverage only intensified after their opening loss. But it was also a triumph for the Australian Rugby League, which chose to cheekily crown the victory as its own after the result was secured. ARL chief executive John Quayle told media after the match:

'Despite being undermined like no other team in Australian Rugby League history, the Kangaroos drew on some good old fashioned Aussie courage to sour the faces of their critics. The ARL regrets many of those critics were Australians.'

This courageous new international competition struck a chord with many who witnessed it. Norman Tasker summarised the impact of Lindsay's spectacularly successful event in *Rugby League Week* magazine, pointing to the new world of rugby league, new nations and the looming promise of Super League. This World Cup was about the bright, sun-filled future of rugby league and finally including other nations to make it more universal. The Australians could celebrate, yet the Kiwis and the English knew they weren't far away either. Just as important, Tonga, Western Samoa and Wales also gave great accounts of themselves.

Scoreboard: **Australia 30** (Steve Menzies 2, Tim Brasher, Mark Coyne, Brad Fittler, Terry Hill tries; Andrew Johns 3 goals) defeated **New Zealand 20** (Richie Barnett, Kevin Iro, Tony Iro tries; Matthew Ridge 4 goals). Crowd: 16,608.

Match 8, 2000

HEARTACHES, FAIRY TALES AND MONSTERS

Australia v. New Zealand

25 November 2000
Old Trafford, Manchester, England
World Cup final

AUSTRALIA	NEW ZEALAND
1. Darren Lockyer	1. Richie Barnett (captain)
2. Wendell Sailor	2. Nigel Vagana
3. Matthew Gidley	3. Tonie Carroll
4. Adam MacDougall	4. Willie Talau
5. Mat Rogers	5. Lesley Vainikolo
6. Brad Fittler (captain)	6. Henry Paul
7. Brett Kimmorley	7. Stacey Jones
8. Shane Webcke	8. Craig Smith
9. Andrew Johns	9. Richard Swain
10. Robbie Kearns	10. Quentin Pongia
11. Gorden Tallis	11. Matt Rua
12. Bryan Fletcher	12. Stephen Kearney
13. Scott Hill	13. Ruben Wiki
Interchange:	Interchange:
14. Trent Barrett	14. Robbie Paul
15. Nathan Hindmarsh	15. Joe Vagana
16. Darren Britt	16. Nathan Cayless
17. Jason Stevens	17. Logan Swann
Coach: Bob Fulton	Coach: Frank Endacott

Referee: Stuart Cummings

Twelve-year-old Richie Barnett tied his shoelaces. It was 5.30 in the morning and he was about to go for a run, something he did three times a week in winter. He read with interest about Australian rugby league players and how they trained to become the best in the world. Following in the footsteps of the Aussies, early runs, swimming and other cross-training exercises became part of his routine. That all-round sporting background at such a young age would serve him well when, as the New Zealand captain many years later, he would suffer injuries so bad that most players would have given the game away altogether.

Stadium Australia, Sydney, Thursday, 27 April 2000. The Kiwis were playing the Kangaroos in that year's Anzac Test. Barnett was celebrating his twenty-ninth birthday that day too. New Zealand was suffering on the scoreboard after a difficult preparation of only a few days. Barnett watched on from fullback as the rampant Australians put on a rugby league blitzkrieg.

In the sixty-sixth minute, with the Kangaroos leading 34–0, hulking Australian winger Wendell Sailor chased a grubber kick aimed for the New Zealand goal-line. It was at this point that Barnett's birthday celebrations ended in a pool of blood.

As the ball bobbled in the Kiwis' in-goal area, Barnett slowed down to collect it and prevent any chance of a Kangaroo try. But Sailor kept his eye on the ball too, running at full pace. Then it happened. Whack. Sailor's forehead collided with the side of Barnett's face. Both players reeled back from the impact. It was like a truck hitting a hatchback head-on. Whereas the truck, Sailor, was able to shake it off with only a scratch, the hatchback was a complete write-off. The New Zealand captain would take six months to recover from injuries that doctors would later liken to those from a car crash.

Barnett was in sheer agony. Blood was pouring from his nose. He couldn't lift his head up or even open his eyes. Barnett had received his fair share of knocks. A rugby league fullback is usually the smallest player and is heavily targeted by opposition players in attack and defence. This time it was off the charts. The Aucklander left the field in a medicab clutching his face. It was in the Stadium Australia changing rooms that the extent of the damage became gruesomely real.

I remember Peter Leitch putting his hands on my jaw.
All the people around me flinched back as he did. They
heard my jaw crack multiple times. After getting into an

Richie Barnett came back from a horrific collision with Wendell Sailor to lead the Kiwis in the World Cup later that year. It remains one of international rugby league's greatest stories of courage. Photosport

ambulance, I was given morphine to relieve the pain. I can tell you it did absolutely nothing at all.

Once at the hospital, Barnett's face swelled up and the bleeding continued for another two hours which prevented the doctors from operating. Those comparisons to a highway crash were accurate: he suffered ten fractures to his cheekbone, a fractured eye socket, a broken nose and broken jaw. He was in intensive care for a week and had a tracheotomy inserted in his throat to help his breathing.

His doctors told him he would never play again.

That cold diagnosis could have easily meant many dark days, and there were a few of those, yet the headstrong Barnett decided on taking it day-by-day to recover. He began to eat, then his throat started to heal. Some basic exercise came next, although he still had real fear over jolting his face after titanium plates were inserted. After a few months, he started to put on weight – having lost fifteen kilograms through his inability to eat properly – and began working out at the gym.

The chance of actually playing rugby league again became more of a reality when Kiwis coach Frank Endacott asked if he might be available for the World Cup a few months later. His transformation from hospital patient to international sportsman was complete. It was during the pre-World Cup training camp that his dedication came through.

Barnett triumphed in all the exercise tests and was proclaimed the Kiwis' fittest player. He was in the best physical shape of his life. From being bedridden and in rehab for so many months, it was an incredible story of mental toughness. Still, the psychological scars remained before the first World Cup match against Lebanon.

> Two weeks leading up to the game I didn't sleep. I was
> dreading it. I had real doubts about contact to my face.
> I also realised that I needed to be an inspiration for the
> others, particularly our younger players.

In freezing conditions in Gloucester, England, Barnett threw himself into everything and was named player of the match. The individual accolade aside, he felt relief more than anything else. Barnett's comeback to reach the World Cup served to inspire the entire New Zealand squad – and the rugby league fraternity. Now, it was a case of trying to win the World Cup.

Picking up the international pieces

By the time the new Rugby League International Federation had been launched in 1998, the rugby league world looked very different. The divided competitions involving Super League and the Australian Rugby League in 1997 caused serious issues not only for Test football but domestically too. That year was a farce. It shouldn't be taken seriously. Here's why.

Australian fans and coaches often boast that they could field at least a couple of teams at international level, such is their country's dominance. In 1997, it actually happened.

That season had both Australian Rugby League and News Limited-controlled Super League competitions running in parallel with each other. Whereas the Australian Super League team (full of players who had signed up to this organisation), coached by John Lang, played matches against New Zealand and Great Britain, the Australian Rugby League-aligned national side, coached by Bob Fulton, were left without any proper competition. Their only matches were against Fiji, Papua New Guinea and a Rest of the World team. These were examples of those teams who played that year:

Australia (Super League) v New Zealand	Australia v Rest of the World
Friday 25 April 1997	Friday 11 July 1997
David Peachey	Tim Brasher
Ken Nagas	Mark Coyne
Andrew Ettingshausen	Paul McGregor
Ryan Girdler	Terry Hill
Wendell Sailor	Robbie O'Davis
Laurie Daley (captain)	Brad Fittler (captain)
Allan Langer	Geoff Toovey
Glenn Lazarus	Paul Harragon
Craig Gower	Andrew Johns
Rodney Howe	Mark Carroll
Brad Thorn	Steve Menzies
David Furner	Gary Larson
Darren Smith	Billy Moore
Interchange:	Interchange:
Paul Green	Matt Sing
Julian O'Neill	John Simon
Solomon Haumono	Nik Kosef
Matt Adamson	Dean Pay
Coach: John Lang	Coach: Bob Fulton

These two teams illustrated how much depth Australia had but also the parlous state of Test football in 1997.

International rugby league needed a united front, and quickly. So when Wakefield businessman Sir Rodney Walker took over as RLIF chairman from Maurice Lindsay, the newly formed International Board replaced the Super League International one and returned the worldwide government of the game back to the national bodies.

With a new agenda and big goals, Walker set about creating the world's biggest international rugby league tournament ever: the 2000 World Cup.

Breaking new ground

By late 2000, Australia looked to be far ahead of anyone else in the world. They smashed New Zealand 52–0 and racked up record scores against the world's number two side, England, the year before. France was well behind all of them. It didn't matter. Walker was bullish about what he and new chief executive Neil Tunnicliffe wanted to achieve.

> We thought that with rugby league doing fairly well in the UK at the time, we'd use the tournament as a means of expanding the sport around the country. Instead of staging most of the events in and around the north of England, we took some of the games into Wales where they were trying to grow the game, as well as Northern Ireland and Scotland.

Sounds ambitious? It was. Here's some context. The combined number of rugby league players in Wales, Scotland and Northern Ireland at the time would probably fit into a small apartment block in Sydney. Rugby league in Scotland only started officially in 1997, Welsh rugby league had essentially disbanded after the 1995 World Cup, and Irish rugby league development was still at embryo stage.

Two men were tasked to deliver the World Cup from an operational and marketing perspective. Neal Coupland, Media and Marketing Director, along with Operations Manager Jason Harborow came in with strong professional backgrounds. They only had eighteen months to deliver the biggest rugby league tournament ever planned. Coupland painted a picture of a challenging environment.

> Firstly, we were incredibly short of time to put something like this tournament together. Secondly, we didn't have the level of resources needed to deliver: only four full-time staff. The biggest hurdle was the difficulties the Rugby Football League faced at the end of 1999 and 2000. They were short of cash and had financial pressures from the clubs and staff. While all this was going on, we in the World Cup team were seen as the shining beacon, expanding the game into new areas for a new millennium, but were also constantly under pressure to deliver.

Coupland focused his marketing efforts on those matches held at what he called 'The Big Three' stadiums, namely

Cardiff, Old Trafford and Twickenham. He also brought in a host of new sponsors that helped change rugby league's image in a positive way.

> Rugby league's sponsors had always been beer, cigarettes or alcohol. To bring in sponsors like Emirates, Motorola and Posthouse was tremendous. Having airlines and telecommunications companies on board helped change the profile of rugby league, something that is important even today.

Walker and Coupland appealed to the media and public in the cities of Glasgow, Edinburgh, Belfast and Dublin to get behind their national teams. There was a major problem, though. The public weren't interested. With no major local competitions to draw from, Scotland and Ireland were full of expats with Aussie and English twangs, who wouldn't know a glen from a loch, and thought a shamrock was a type of music. The local press refused to support what they thought was a complete farce; the punters quickly followed. Walker now agrees some of this ambitious scheduling was a mistake.

> The truth is the games weren't supported. The first game (Scotland versus New Zealand Maori) was played in front of a virtually empty stadium. It was a disappointing start. In hindsight, we should have played more games in the heartland of rugby league, the north of England.

Northern Ireland's sports media trashed the World Cup, exhorting any genuine rugby union supporter to boycott the games because rugby league wasn't the right code.

Enflaming the situation was the case of Republic of Ireland striker Tony Cascarino. He released his autobiography in October 2000, right in time for the rugby league World Cup, admitting he was a 'fake Irishman' and never qualified to represent the Irish soccer side. He played for the national team on the basis of a maternal grandfather from the Irish town of Westport, but revealed this wasn't true. It caused outrage. Imagine then the nation having to stomach the idea that their national rugby league team was full of Englishmen and Aussies. Any small spark of interest they may have had was wiped out in one go.

Scotland's situation was very similar. Coach Shaun McRae shocked everyone by putting together a squad containing NRL and Super League players, but because none spoke like Sean Connery or Billy Connolly they didn't capture the public's hearts or minds. The Scottish public voted with their feet and stayed away: only 2000 people saw their opening match against the New Zealand Maori in Glasgow and just 1579 witnessed their game against Samoa in Edinburgh. Rugby league be damned.

The case for Maori

John Tamihere paced around his hotel room and went through his speech one last time. He was in Paris, in late 1998, for a meeting with the International Board. His objective was simple: as the international delegate for New

Zealand Maori rugby league, he was to explain to the other member nations why a Maori team should get a spot in the World Cup.

Maori weren't new at the sport. They had fashioned a strong record in rugby league internationals, having defeated Australia, Great Britain and France since they sent a team to England in 1908. They made up the majority of the playing population in New Zealand and were a proud sporting people.

Tamihere had strong credentials and every right to feel confident. A lawyer, he was heavily involved in the Maori Land courts and Department of Maori Affairs, and had been a passionate advocate for providing quality health and education services to the Maori people. He'd also had a background in rugby league that stretched back to his childhood, with all eleven siblings playing the sport. In 1992, he had his first taste of sports administration at an elite level, helping run the unsanctioned Pacific Cup tournament that included a number of emerging nations, including Tonga, Samoa, Niue plus a Maori team.

League, with its athletic requirements, appealed to the New Zealand indigenous people right from the beginning. From the 1930s, Maori were regular visitors to the coalmines in the north of England as they looked for different work opportunities. This tough environment bred rugby league in these areas, so it's no wonder Maori were a big hit with the locals.

Since the 1980s, Maori rugby league tournaments had grown into the biggest indigenous sporting events held in New Zealand, with multiple grades and age groups. During the 1990s, Maori competed in the various competitions with emerging Pacific nations and had future Kiwis Ruben Wiki, John Lomax, Richie Barnett and Syd Eru in the Maori side too. The Maori's greatest scalp was their 40–28 defeat of the Great Britain tourists in 1996, breaking an eighty-six-year hoodoo in the process. Several Kiwis who took part in the 2000 World Cup had ties to Maori, like Nathan Cayless and Stacey Jones, both with prominent Maori grandfathers in their respective communities.

There was a strong story to tell the other member nations. Having a Maori team in the World Cup didn't mean they were competing for players with the Kiwis, which was still the national team. Maori needed to have a place at the table.

> The pitch was very clear. We spoke the idea of
> nationhood and our rights to be part of a tournament
> like this. We talked about the Maori Battalion in World
> War I, ... a pioneer battalion [that] paved the way for the
> Maori to fight as their own special unit in World War II.
> By playing in the World Cup it would be a opportunity
> to break further ground, like those battalions did, which
> was also in line with the 'expansionist' vision behind the
> event. We would be representing our people and talked
> about the idea of sovereignty, which the Irish, Scottish
> and Welsh could relate to, having one government
> for different people – a nation within a nation. All
> the member nations agreed eventually, apart from the
> Australians and Papua New Guineans who hesitated, but
> we got them over the line.

Amid much debate mainly in New Zealand, the 'Aotearoa Maori', as they were titled, took their place in the World Cup. It had one spin-off: the New Zealand public took more interest in this event because the country had two teams playing in it.

Upsetting rugby's traditions

If you've ever had the good fortune to attend Lords during a cricket Test match, you'll know what I mean about the unique vibe of the place. It has a special atmosphere that reminds you it is the home of cricket. The bacon-and-egg coloured ties. The members' section full of suited individuals. The polite clapping when runs are scored. Lords will always be synonymous with cricket.

In the same vein, Twickenham Stadium is the home of English rugby union, an association that stretches back more than a century. Sir Rodney Walker decided to smash this whole perception. Along with breaking new ground, pushing boundaries and expanding the countries participating, staging a World Cup match at Twickenham was his gutsiest move.

What would happen if only 20,000 people came? As it turned out, close to 45,000 braved the shocking weather on the opening night and watched as the Kangaroos grounded out a 22–2 win against England. Although the stadium was still only half full, which made it look relatively empty, staging the match here was a high-risk move that needs to be applauded and celebrated for its boldness. London was still a rugby union outpost; Paris, the home of French rugby, also held a double-header.

Despite the bravery shown by a very inexperienced England team that night, the grumbling and negative pro-rugby union journalists sharpened their pens soon after the match ended. In many respects, the attacks by sections of the press throughout the UK smacked of a resistance to change and an unwillingness to look outside their own sporting bubble. Australia's 110-point mauling of Russia and the Kiwis' 84–10 disposal of the Cook Islands fanned the flames of ridicule even more.

A nasty bout of amnesia swept through rugby union's international media during the months of October and November that year, as they seemingly had no recollection of rugby's 1999 World Cup. It was puzzling to think they had forgotten the events of 14 and 15 October, when New Zealand and England racked up century scorelines in the pool stages. Tiny rugby nations like Uruguay, Namibia, Spain and Romania had to face Australia, England, New Zealand and South Africa. Selective memories, jealousy of the other code or indifference; they could all be factors. What we know is that the ambitious nature of the 2000 World Cup meant people couldn't be ambivalent about it.

The Welsh Dragons set the tournament alight again

Grown men cried in the stands. Strangers hugged each other. It wasn't a pub or a counselling session, though. It was the Wales rugby league team's dream-like run to the semi-finals of the World Cup in 1995. One of those grown men – not a fan of rugby league – decided to show what it meant by writing a letter to coach Clive Griffiths personally.

For anyone who read it, this carefully crafted hand-written note told you what an impact the national team's performance had had on the Welsh public consciousness. In Griffiths' decades of coaching, this was the most poignant and memorable act he had ever seen.

For a non-rugby league fan to express such delight should have been enough to demonstrate the potential of Welsh rugby league at that time. But the Rugby Football League and International Board didn't capitalise on the nation's biggest moment in the sport since the 1975 World Cup. According to Griffiths, who was key in getting Welsh rugby league back on an accelerated path, both organisations let them down. Horribly.

> We had lots of meetings but nothing happened. The
> RFL didn't bite the bullet. We had a real platform to
> capitalise on Welsh rugby league with all the interest we
> had from that tournament. As an example, a group of
> 10,000 Welsh fans went to Old Trafford [for the semi-
> final] to support us.

This sensational side, a team that gelled so well together that Griffiths frequently referred to it as a 'club', quietly disbanded. A couple of Tests against France and England in 1996 appeased some quarters, but then Wales disappeared off the international radar. For a team that were World Cup semi-finalists a year earlier, they had to wait two years before they played another Test. In 1998, they played only one, against England. Sixteen months later, Wales had two

Tests in the space of a week – one each against Ireland and Scotland, both brand-new nations to rugby league. Wales lost both. From regularly finding the try-line against France and Western Samoa a few years earlier, they couldn't beat Europe's international rookies. It was heart-breaking, scandalous and plain wrong. It also reflected Australia's and England's focus on their own domestic competitions at the time. There were also two international boards: the Super League and the official one. The international game was shunted to the back of the queue.

With Super League introduced into the English rugby league scene in 1996, in came new hope too. A team from South Wales was mooted to join the expanded competition. The promise never turned into reality and it collapsed. With those hopes dashed, players had to remain playing for English club sides; Griffiths opted to coach Great Britain in 1996 and also had stints in the rugby union ranks.

In 1998, he was asked to coach the team again in preparation for the next World Cup. But whereas in 1995 he could count on experienced rugby union players with a sprinkling of great league talent, the market had changed. Rugby union went professional and suddenly there was a dearth of cross-coding superstars to call up to bolster the Welsh team. Griffiths had to build a new team, with few resources and little time.

Only Iestyn Harris, Anthony Sullivan and Keiron Cunningham remained from the 1995 semi-final team. Paul Moriarty and John Devereux were asked to come out of retirement to play, four years after they'd hung up their boots! For the 2000 campaign, Griffiths was forced to choose seven players who had never played for Wales or even at international level. It was only through the magic touch he brought to getting his 'band' back together and instilling pride and passion into the Dragons jersey that they were able to pass through a tough pool group relatively unscathed. New Zealand outclassed them, but they entered a semi-final against Australia with absolutely nothing to lose, odds of 100–1 against them, and a smile on their faces. It was the Toyota Corolla versus a fleet of Ferraris.

This sporting underdog story had a later equivalent: Crawley Town's FA Cup match against Manchester United in 2011. But whereas Crawley had a big-spending owner, the Wales rugby league team had nothing of the kind. Five-eighth Lee Briers revealed in his autobiography that he won more money in a game of cards on tour in 2005 than he ever did playing for Wales.

Unlike Crawley Town, which couldn't score a goal against the Red Devils, the Welsh rugby league team piled on the points in a rapid-fire first half. Australia could only shake their heads in shock. The millionaires were left spinning; the pensioners had a real chance of winning.

The Kangaroos started powerfully with two unconverted tries to Brett Kimmorley and Wendell Sailor. But Wales earned a gritty try to halfback Ian Watson, who carried Australian fullback Darren Lockyer literally on his back to score underneath the uprights. It was one of those poetic moments in sport. Lockyer was probably still celebrating his Clive Churchill Medal (the NRL grand final player of the match) and was in his prime as a fullback. Watson had completed a season with second-tier club Swinton. Lockyer wasn't wearing his medal that night, though.

Wales kept trying their luck. A fortuitous pass from Briers bounced into the hands of centre Kris Tassell, who charged through a big gap between Sailor and Lockyer to score. Harris converted the angled kick to give the Dragons a 12–8 lead. Griffiths was up off the bench on the side-line but didn't allow himself to smile. That moment would come very soon.

Next came the stuff of dreams. Harris launched a huge kick in the centre of the field, aimed at Lockyer who was isolated at fullback. As often with these spiralling bombs, time seemed to stand still. Lockyer would have practised taking these high kicks a hundred times during the season, in warm-ups, during games and at practice. He hardly had to move. With the crowd watching, he shuffled slightly, quite casually, then leapt as high as he could from a stationary position.

The only Welsh player chasing was little Lee Briers. His eyes never left the football. With the poise of a long-jump athlete, the Welsh five-eighth leapt off the ground and clattered into Lockyer in mid-air. The timing was perfect. Briers managed to rip the ball out from Lockyer's hands, turn and land with only Australia's in-goal to greet him. It happened that quickly.

What joy. Briers finished by launching a child-like jumping dive and placed the ball over the try-line. A more circumspect or nervous team might have concentrated on just getting the ball over safely. This wasn't Wales. Briers jumped in jubilation and his teammates engulfed him in an impromptu group celebration. Griffiths, after keeping his emotions in check for so long, allowed himself an unhinged, delighted celebration. 'Somebody pinch me, I'm dreaming,' a stunned Eddie Hemmings said in television commentary.

More penalties by Harris and two long-range drop goals from Briers meant Wales earned a 20–14 lead at half-time. Hemmings, normally so verbose and full of adjectives, was speechless. This story didn't end well for the underdog, though, as Australia found their attack in the second half, finishing with a 46–22 victory and a place in the World Cup final. Wales had reduced the world champions to a confused mess for sixty minutes, something no other opponent could do in that tournament. Their twenty-two points was the most scored against the Kangaroos since the Kiwis' 22–24 loss in the 1999 Tri-Nations final, seven Tests previously.

Welsh rugby league could have kicked on to great heights. They had such a great base as Wales were the only team to make the semi-finals of the 1995 and 2000 World Cups. But it didn't happen. Again. The man who featured so prominently in the latter campaign, Lee Briers, vented his frustration in his book: 'Wales dropped away after 1995 and 2000. It was f---king scandalous. We had the base to grow from and it wasn't taken advantage of.'

The lack of development in the emerging nations would be a constant theme over the next decade.

Kiwis flying high

Over in the other semi-final, New Zealand put England to the sword in a record 49–6 drubbing of the home team. Hip flasks were passed around in the media box such was the depression felt by the home press about England's performance. The English had a young side, but their coach Phil Larder had no excuses, calling the Kiwis' performance 'a bit special' in the press conference afterwards.

Kiwis coach Frank Endacott told me he felt the most confident he'd ever been against Australia going into the World Cup final. He'd had a strong build-up, a good squad and an experienced team. Endacott had got used to the feeling of beating Australia and liked it. He'd overseen wins in 1997, 1998 and 1999, with the closest of losses in the Tri–Nations final the previous year. The 2000 Anzac Test blowout needed to be viewed in isolation for what it was: an ambush. With greater preparation and more games together, this Kiwis side was primed to finally break the Australian hold on World Cup finals.

The Raging Bull and the Warhorse

You saw his eyes first. They stuck out at you, angry for no reason other than you happened to be the opposition. Then the snarl, as if gritting his teeth ready for the tackle he's about to dish out. Finally, it's his giant 1.89 metre, 108 kilogram frame, stooping slightly as if tired from clobbering blokes on the footy field each week. Gorden Tallis redefined forward play for his generation, using his raw power and sheer energy to intimidate the opposition. Although his time in an Australian jersey was a relatively short one, he became the mainstay of the Kangaroo's forward pack and a symbol of their dominance in the late 1990s and early 2000s.

As a youngster entering the Australian first-grade competition, his role was initially off the bench to create an impact. Coaches marvelled at how he created an intensity that few matched on the football field. Tallis spoke in his autobiography about working himself into a frenzy during training sessions, often imagining situations and players so he could operate at maximum capacity. Whereas his colleagues would relax and have a laugh, Tallis would turn up his energy levels to simulate match day.

Firebrands still belong in rugby league. They are made for the game. Not everyone can ghost through the game like Darren Lockyer, using his natural skills. Tallis had an energy and intimidation ability with and without the ball. This unyielding commitment to his teams got him into trouble on occasion with administrators, opposition coaches and even referees.

One moment in Tallis's career is particularly jarring. State of Origin, Game 1, a few weeks after the 2000 Anzac Test. Tallis was having a running dialogue with referee Bill Harrigan, providing a critique of his performance as the match wore on. In the last fifteen minutes, New South Wales centre Ryan Girdler scored a try after what looked like a couple of knock-ons by his teammates earlier in the tackle count. As Girdler was celebrating, Tallis went over to Harrigan and called him a cheat on several occasions. The referee sent him off in a moment that lives on in infamy for many rugby league fans. There was plenty of pride, passion and energy that day – but would he be too much of a risk in a World Cup knock-out game?

Australian coach Chris Anderson had no qualms about picking the big forward. He held him in such high esteem that not only did he select Tallis for the World Cup but he also made him captain for one of the pool matches against Russia. Tallis responded by scoring four tries. Anderson felt that although he had previous history with referees, the big forward had earned the right to be the Australian skipper. Tallis was so delighted with the honour that he dedicated two chapters in his autobiography to the World Cup and what it meant to be the Kangaroos' captain.

Fellow Queensland forward Shane Webcke deserves much of the praise for keeping Australia's record so flawless during this period. After master coach Wayne Bennett watched him play a game of 'park football', as Webcke termed it, he had a rapid rise through the professional ranks. Webcke made his international debut in 1997, like Tallis, and built a reputation as a hard-working, consistent, unrelenting forward for club, state and country. Whereas Tallis provided the gusto on the edge of the ruck, Webcke saw his role as much simpler.

Up front, our role was to advance the football.
Particularly at Test level, the key was about getting good momentum and to win the early exchanges. If you could get quick play of the balls so the next man can get a little extra, he does the same and gets a little more, then it would pay off in the long run.

As Mat Rogers kicked off to start the World Cup final, you can bet those early exchanges were the only things going through the minds of Webcke, Tallis and the other forwards. The Kiwis reacted in surprise at the speed and intensity of the Australians, who zoned in on their opponents like magnets.

Tallis was in first. Running at top speed, he smashed his shoulder into Kiwi prop Craig Smith, back-flipping him hard into the Wembley turf. Webcke took it upon himself to do better next tackle, slamming into Quentin Pongia. On tackle three, Tallis timed his run perfectly, driving Ruben Wiki backwards. The Kiwis were spooked. Their first three tackles only gained fifteen metres. New Zealand five-eighth Henry Paul put a wobbly kick in and the Australians packed down for a scrum on halfway. Webcke and Tallis knew they had made their presence felt.

Battle of the halfbacks

In an era where Australia could choose five quality Test halfbacks, Brett Kimmorley was the incumbent for six years. After winning an NRL premiership with the Melbourne Storm, which was also coached by Anderson, Kimmorley slotted into the Kangaroo set-up easily. His running game and superlative kicking skills – in particular his array of short kicks, grubbers and bombs – freed up the likes of Wendell Sailor and Mat Rogers to score tries or take advantage of poor opposition defence. He was also a strong runner who could break the defensive line.

New Zealand couldn't boast such depth. For a decade there was only one man: Stacey Jones. Grandson of 1950s

Kiwis prop Maunga Emery, Jones was even smaller than Kimmorley (1.71 to the Australian's 1.73 metres tall), yet like his Australian rival he was the complete package on the football field. He had great vision, a superb kicking game and, when needed, had real acceleration off the mark. Both halfbacks had been in great form throughout the World Cup, with only the final left. Whereas Jones shared the playmaking duties with Henry Paul – a gifted and creative player in his own right – Kimmorley could call upon four attacking options at any one time: Darren Lockyer at fullback, Brad Fittler at five-eighth, Andrew Johns at hooker and Trent Barrett on the bench.

Johns is acknowledged as Australia's greatest ever halfback, yet he played hooker for half of his Test career. This often gets lost in analysis and is an extraordinary fact – but it speaks volumes for his impact at club and state level. Kimmorley had special praise for two of his play-making colleagues.

> Darren Lockyer and Andrew Johns are the only two
> players in my whole career who had an aura about them.
> I was always fairly confident with those two in the side.
> With Johns, he could create through ad lib football too.

The Kiwis would have loved a Johns or a Lockyer. As was often the case with the Kiwis during the late 1990s, it was usually down to Jones and maybe Matthew Ridge, Richie Barnett or Henry Paul to share the kicking duties. The same happened in the World Cup final. Kimmorley and

Fittler took turns peppering the New Zealanders through some testing kicks, with only desperate defence holding the Kangaroos out. It took Australia half an hour to open the scoring, Sailor putting in a low kick through for Matthew Gidley to beat Stephen Kearney and score. Rogers converted from the side-line for a 6–0 lead. It remained that way at half-time. Barnett also almost repeated his accident with Sailor – this time, the kick bounced into touch.

Despite tries by Tonie Carroll and Lesley Vainikolo in the second half, Australia put their foot down and the Kiwis couldn't respond. The 40–12 score suggests a hammering; in truth, New Zealand was only six points down with fifteen minutes to play. It was another personal triumph for

Australia celebrate winning the 2000 World Cup. Rugby League Journal

the superb, ageless Brad Fittler, who had played in three winning World Cup teams since 1992.

As the Australians celebrated, Richie Barnett was as forlorn as the other Kiwis: head down, hands on hips, crestfallen. However, he had won his own battle despite New Zealand ending up in second place. He felt sorrow and pain, yet he had climbed his own personal Mount Everest that year by getting back to full health.

In the changing rooms, Ruben Wiki spontaneously presented Frank Endacott with his Kiwi jersey and Stephen Kearney gave a heartfelt speech. There was a lot of emotion in the room for 'Happy Frank', who had announced it was to be his last game as New Zealand coach.

Was it Wendell?

Neal Coupland wiped the sweat from his brow. He was under pressure. Television crews from the BBC and Sky Sports wanted to know the official World Cup final Man of the Match so they could tell their millions of viewers.

Forty members of the press needed to cast their votes. This took time, a commodity Coupland didn't have. Finally, his television floor manager received an ultimatum to confirm who the winner was.

The votes hadn't been finalised. It didn't matter. He guessed that Wendell Sailor was the winner. The television audience heard this. A few minutes later, Coupland counted the votes. As the Australian winger walked off the platform with the award in his hand and a big grin on his face, Coupland nervously looked at the result. Wendell Sailor had won.

Like this near-gaffe, not everything in the 2000 World Cup had gone to plan. Commercially, the event wasn't deemed a success. Relentless rain kept people away and public transport issues made travelling less appealing. The build-up wasn't ideal and the tournament team lacked budget and staff.

All wasn't lost, though. The tournament gave France a much-needed jolt of rugby league exposure. In the United Kingdom, it is thanks to the World Cup tournament that rugby league is a much more widely acknowledged sport and it is now played in the armed forces and in universities. Airlines and telecommunications sectors came into the sport as sponsors. Telstra, First Utility and Webjet now play key roles in the NRL and Super League.

Sir Rodney Walker admitted the 2000 World Cup would always disappoint him. Yet the tournament shouldn't go down in history as a backward step for international rugby league. Walker was one of rugby league's 'brave hearts': someone who dared to be different, taking the game out of the sport's heartlands for the first time on a grand scale. Rugby league fans around the world should thank him for having had the courage to do so.

Scoreboard: **Australia 40** (Wendell Sailor 2, Trent Barrett, Brad Fittler, Matthew Gidley, Nathan Hindmarsh, Darren Lockyer tries; Mat Rogers 6 goals) defeated **New Zealand 12** (Tonie Carroll, Lesley Vainikolo tries; Henry Paul 2 goals). Crowd: 44,329.

Match 9, 2008

'THE BLACK AND WHITE BALL IS UNDERWAY'

Australia v. New Zealand

23 November 2008
Suncorp Stadium, Brisbane, Australia
World Cup final

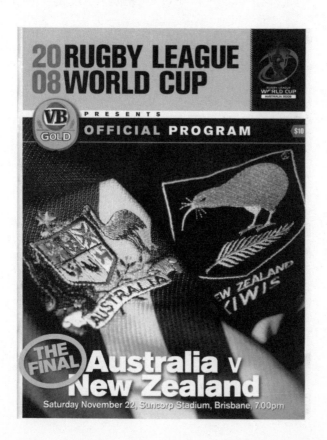

AUSTRALIA	NEW ZEALAND
1. Billy Slater	1. Lance Hohaia
2. Joel Monaghan	2. Sam Perrett
3. Greg Inglis	3. Simon Mannering
4. Israel Folau	4. Jerome Ropati
5. David Williams	5. Manu Vatuvei
6. Darren Lockyer (captain)	6. Benji Marshall
7. Johnathan Thurston	7. Nathan Fien
8. Brent Kite	8. Nathan Cayless (captain)
9. Cameron Smith	9. Thomas Leuluai
10. Petero Civoniceva	10. Adam Blair
11. Anthony Laffranchi	11. David Fa'alogo
12. Glenn Stewart	12. Bronson Harrison
13. Paul Gallen	13. Jeremy Smith
Interchange:	Interchange:
14. Karmichael Hunt	14. Issac Luke
15. Anthony Tupou	15. Greg Eastwood
16. Craig Fitzgibbon	16. Sam Rapira
17. Anthony Watmough	17. Sika Manu
Coach: Ricky Stuart	Coach: Stephen Kearney

Referee: Ashley Klein

Gary Kemble's world fell apart on 14 January 2008. New Zealand's rugby league coach had no indication that this would be anything else but a relaxing afternoon after a couple of months touring in the UK and France. It was a warm summer's day in Brisbane. But in Auckland, storm clouds were forming.

When Kiwis captain Roy Asotasi used a press conference to declare he had no faith in Kemble, it took journalists, punters and his employers by complete surprise. After all, an early pre-season training session shouldn't have contained any dark secrets other than an update on injuries or fitness sessions. But there he was, on a summer's afternoon, stating that he and his team didn't think his coach was good enough to lead them into the World Cup at the year's end.

This dramatic moment completed one of the darkest chapters in New Zealand sport. Most players saved their pot shots for retirement or juicy autobiographies. But here was the current New Zealand skipper questioning the abilities of his coach without fear of retribution. It amounted to sporting treason.

Was it courageous, selfless or in bad taste? Maybe a bit of all three. But one thing was for certain: Asotasi didn't like what he saw from the new coach and wanted instant change. If this coup worked, then perhaps Kemble could go before the tournament started.

He certainly had evidence to go on. Savaged by Australia and Great Britain on their end-of-year tour in 2007, a young Kiwis team struggled to adapt to Kemble's mentorship on the park. Off it, there were reported stories about sex scandals, inter-team fighting and bizarre coaching sessions, all smeared across the national newspapers. Even the most hardened Kiwi supporters were turning off in disbelief.

Six months earlier, the popular incumbent, Brian McClennan, had announced that he wanted to keep his Kiwis job but also take up a full-time role with the Leeds Rhinos. The New Zealand Rugby League said no, as they insisted their coach resided in the country. But for that to happen, the list of available candidates – an already very small pool – reduced even more. By this reckoning, the Kiwis coach would need to be either the New Zealand Warriors coach, or coaching in the local, largely amateur provincial competition. Yes, McClennan had brought success, but to use a non-NRL coach was a big gamble. Gary Kemble replaced him.

His appointment should have been a shining example for the New Zealand Rugby League's coaching pathways. A Kiwis fullback in the 1980s, Kemble had progressed across the coaching ranks at all levels, from club, Junior Kiwis, reserve grade, NRL and international roles. He'd learned from the likes of Frank Endacott and Daniel Anderson, prepared the Kiwis in the 1995 World Cup and served time at the New Zealand Warriors. Privately, he was excited by his appointment, but publicly, the New Zealand sports media seemed hell-bent on taking him down.

All coaches want to start their tenure on a positive note. How about New Zealand's worst loss in a hundred years? That's what Kemble's Kiwis delivered against a young Australian team at Westpac Stadium in Wellington. You could hear the journalists high-fiving in delight as they crafted the headlines. Bad news sells. But there was more: a reported 'sex scandal' that was, according to Kemble, blown way out of proportion. But the media grabbed onto it with glee.

It got much worse. An experienced Great Britain team pushed the greenhorn Kiwis around in all three Tests. The series ended up a whitewash for the home team, the worst since 1993: 14–20, 0–44 and 22–28. New Zealand's young players – the squad's average age was twenty-two – showed glimpses of their raw talent, leading Britain early in the first and third Tests. Yet it was the second match, when the side posted New Zealand's worst loss to the Lions, that the media focused on. A close win against the French in Paris ended the tour on a small high. Sensing the pressure building around him, Kemble decided to call a frank meeting with his captain. It was here, in a café in Paris, that he had a heart-to-heart with Asotasi. How was he feeling? What about the players? Kemble remembers asking his skipper a direct question during the hour-long conversation.

Kemble: 'Do you think I am good enough?'

'Yes,' Asotasi replied.

Kemble flew back to New Zealand, feeling relieved after clearing the air with his skipper. A month later, Asotasi gave his press conference. Kemble came out fighting in response, defending his role and pledging his commitment to turning the results around. When I spoke to him a few years later, Kemble felt like the sports press had a personal agenda to take him down.

The media were on a mission to bring me down right from the start. Everything was blown out of proportion. The so-called 'sex scandal' was nothing of the sort. One of the girls was a cousin of the players. But a father who was there heard something and then took it to the media who took it way out of context. There was another story about the players serving drinks as waiters without shirts on. That was just a game they played between themselves! Every little thing was focused on. We couldn't believe it.

Whichever side you took, and whatever stories you believed, the team results simply weren't good enough. Both Kemble and Asotasi needed to take responsibility for the on-field performances. In the harsh light of reality, the captain and coach needed to take a hard look at themselves. Were they both the right people for the job?

The drama didn't last long. Kemble resigned a week after Asotasi's admonishing. Less than a year out from the World Cup, New Zealand all of a sudden had no leadership: their coach got fired and the captain was under disciplinary review. There was only one option left to save the Kiwis and their shot at the World Cup. He was a lanky, former policeman from Queensland, considered the greatest coach of his generation.

Luring the master

It wouldn't be easy. To bring Wayne Bennett onto the New Zealand coaching staff would have been unthinkable only three years earlier. After all, the Kiwis had ended Bennett's Kangaroo coaching stint after their Tri-Nations final victory. Yet a couple of crucial factors worked in the Kiwis' favour. Firstly, Bennett took an active interest in the health of Test rugby league. With the Kiwis struggling, it meant international rugby league's brand suffered. And if that happened, the upcoming World Cup's credibility suffered too. This tournament needed to go well – and Australia needed to be tested – if rugby league wanted to grow on the world stage. It had been eight long years since the last one; the other nations hadn't been considered fit enough to match the Australians.

You could say that Bennett got into coaching by chance as he initially wanted to coach so he could develop young people. He furthered this ability after spending time as a mentor to junior officers in the police force. After working with the Queensland Rugby League, the Brisbane Broncos offered him their inaugural head coach role. Twenty-one years and six premierships later, Bennett still enjoyed the satisfaction of developing younger players into better people.

In the 1990s, during a time when most first-grade coaches were selfishly looking after their own club's interests, the Queenslander actively encouraged his players to play for their country. Australian Rugby League chairman Colin Love was appreciative of his support, particularly during the 'Super League war' when international rugby league was almost obliterated. Bennett always saw the big picture.

Bennett led the push for the Tri-Nations tournament to be reinstated in 2004. That year he became the Australian coach for the second time, after performing the role for two matches in 1998. He wanted his Kangaroos to be a consistent team and felt it didn't happen during his time in charge, so he resigned after the Kiwis' 24–0 win in the Tri-Nations final. He decided to spend more time with his Broncos.

New Zealand Rugby League chairman Ray Haffenden had the job of luring the master coach across. He took a 6am flight to Brisbane and travelled deep into regional Queensland to meet Bennett at his farm. There were no suits, no contracts and no meeting rooms; the job offer happened in the Bennett family kitchen after his wife Trish brought in a plate of sandwiches.

Haffenden then asked Bennett if he'd like to coach the Kiwis.

'Wayne initially said no. He felt strongly that a New Zealander should coach the Kiwis. He was, however, happy to help out in an assistant capacity or some other way.'

This wasn't in the script. Bennett was supposed to agree to the top job with Stephen Kearney as his assistant. The decision on whether Wayne Bennett would sign with New Zealand now lay in the hands of Kearney. Securing the biggest coaching coup in Kiwi rugby league history suddenly looked shaky. Kearney had to agree to work with Bennett – plus be comfortable running the show with his assistance. Haffenden felt nervous, as he needed an answer from the former New Zealand captain quickly. Bennett wasn't a man to mess around.

Kearney had forged an impeccable reputation as a true professional during his lengthy playing career. With more than

ten years in the national team and almost 300 NRL and Super
League matches, he also remained the youngest ever Kiwis
captain, at twenty-one years old. Even while playing junior
football in both rugby union and league, former coaches
would remark at how studiously he approached his tasks.

Kearney wanted time to weigh up the options. But
Haffenden told him he only had five minutes to make a
decision. Kearney had his own concerns. These weren't
anything to do with working with the veteran coach. The
New Zealand Rugby League had struggled financially for
as long as anyone could remember. Signing the super-coach
would push the national body into even greater debt. Was it
a small mercy to get international football, and the Kiwis,
back to a competitive level in a World Cup year?

In the end, Kearney agreed. Bennett did too. So, very
proudly, on 11 February 2008, NZRL officials named
Stephen Kearney as new head coach with Wayne Bennett
his assistant. The duo had less than nine months to prepare
for the World Cup, and less than two before a Test against
Australia. After months of headlines and heartache, it was
back to the business of winning football matches.

A new blueprint

Colin Love had one aim for the 2008 World Cup:
commercial success. A true visionary in the sport, he created
the inaugural World Sevens tournament as far back the
late 1980s, allowing the likes of Japan and Lebanon to play
rugby league in a gentle setting. Men like Maurice Lindsay
and Sir Rodney Walker expanded these concepts at World

Cup level, but Love, a long-standing Australian Rugby League chairman, had the gumption to test it out in these developmental competitions.

He hadn't enjoyed the previous two World Cups. Love told me that the ARL had to chase to get their share of the revenue from the 1995 event, even commencing litigation until the Rugby Football League finally paid at the eleventh hour. He was also a frustrated bystander at the 2000 World Cup, watching as the massive debts incurred meant the developing nations couldn't get access to much-needed funds. When he became the 2008 World Cup tournament director, he had twenty years' worth of ideas to put into practice.

Love wanted to create a blueprint for other World Cups to copy. His team developed a proper line of merchandising, a distinctive logo and trademarks too, with much of the cost underwritten by the New South Wales and Queensland governments. As a result, the tournament generated a heart-warming $6 million in revenue. The world body could finally invest in the developing nations, as well as expand the Tri-Nations (featuring Australia, New Zealand and Great Britain) into a Four Nations tournament, which would include an alternating northern then southern hemisphere team to get exposure to the 'Big Three'.

Ricky's redemption

While the Kiwis set about rebuilding their new coaching team, Ricky Stuart had quietly moulded a high-performing Kangaroos side over the previous two years. He'd crafted an impressive playing career as a halfback, guiding Australia to a last-minute series win in the 1990 Kangaroos tour and achieving great success at club and state level. He was never satisfied with simply playing the game: his thirst for knowledge, strategies and philosophies about rugby league continued well after his retirement.

He played under some of the very best coaches of his era; Tim Sheens, Phil Gould, Mal Meninga and Jack Gibson all passed on their immense knowledge. Stuart made a natural progression into coaching after retiring, taking the Sydney Roosters to the 2002 NRL premiership in his first year in charge. More success followed and he was invited to coach Australia after Bennett stepped down in December 2005. How did he get his Kangaroos to bounce back after being humiliated by the Kiwis?

He restored pride to the Australian jersey, that's how. Stuart brought in former Kangaroos to share their experiences at Test level; men like Wally Lewis, Gene Miles, Allan Langer and John Cartwright. He wanted his men to cherish the Kangaroos' proud history, and to get the current group to understand their place in Australian rugby league history. The coach's first assignment was the 2006 Anzac Test, which also turned out to be Andrew Johns's last. It shaped up as a revenge mission.

'That was a particularly memorable Test,' Stuart recalled. 'The win was retaliation from the Tri-Nations final loss the year before. It was about getting respect back.'

A 50–12 victory made emphatic headlines, and he continued to build a team of exciting youngsters over the next few seasons, many of these forging outstanding careers for their country, such as Cameron Smith and Johnathan Thurston. Stuart's Kangaroos went into 2008's international season extremely confident after remaining unbeaten against the Kiwis and only suffering a loss to Great Britain in Sydney. Little did they know that New Zealand were about to get some of their inside secrets revealed by a former mentor.

Selling secrets

Wayne Bennett looked forward to working more closely with the Kiwis. He had got a small taste of it before the Kiwis' tour in 2007 as part of an exhibition match and enjoyed the experience. Fast-forward to May 2008, and Australia were taking on New Zealand at the Sydney Cricket Ground. These one-off matches tend to fade from memory quickly given the regular wins by the Kangaroos, yet this one had a moment to remember. At the same time, it showcased Australia's new breed of 'super-athletes'.

Greg Inglis and Israel Folau had quickly become the new poster-boys for rugby league in the modern age: very tall, fast, athletic players who had the ability to out-jump Australian Rules football players. Only minutes into the match, Inglis leapt high in the air outside the in-goal, and in the same motion flung the ball back in play for Mark Gasnier to catch and score a try. It was superhero-like. The Kiwis had no way back. At one point Australia had scored twenty-two points in twenty minutes. They were too fast, too clinical and simply too good. A 28–12 win was galling.

But you wouldn't have guessed that by the Kiwis' reaction after the game. Nathan Cayless, who replaced Asotasi as captain through injury, remembered:

> We got to the changing rooms and were pretty happy,
> it was a fairly jovial atmosphere. Then Wayne walked
> in and gave us a really scathing assessment. He said,
> 'That was very poor. If you were satisfied with that
> performance, I don't want to be part of the World Cup
> with you.'

Bennett spent a week with the Kiwis leading up to that match and allowed them to understand the Kangaroos' philosophy and approach. He had very clear views on why they hadn't achieved sustained success against Australia. New Zealand sides in the past were perceived as happy to get close to a win, whereas the Kangaroos wanted to give teams good hidings. Australians didn't want to just win. Second place wasn't good enough. After the Kiwis' Centenary Test performance, why should the Queenslander continue?

He wanted the World Cup to be a success and for the Kiwis to improve. So he continued in the role. But Bennett made it very clear that he wouldn't tolerate a repeat of that type of performance.

Former coach McClennan started the Kiwis' belief that they could beat the Kangaroos regularly. His coaching was full of slogans, themes, innovation and tactics that caught Australia off-guard in the 2005 Tri-Nations. With only Manu Vatuvei left of that group, someone needed to get them to believe again. With Kearney looking after the technical side of the coaching, Bennett worked on getting a mental edge. It proved to be a powerful combination.

'He was the master of the psychological aspect of sport,' Cayless explained, his beaming smile apparent on the telephone. 'He tells you how good you are, not just the starting team but the whole squad. He made us believe in ourselves and believe we can beat anyone.' New Zealand team manager Dean Bell also shared that the coach's presence alone was beneficial for Kearney and all the team staff.

Forwards Jeremy Smith and Adam Blair brought in a hard-nosed, hard-working ethos from their Melbourne Storm experience. Home truths came out during the training sessions. Bonds formed. Blokes were in tears. Players revealed personal sacrifices that the whole group understood. A culture of honesty was born.

Getting past the white wall

The World Cup organisers hailed England's pool match against Australia in Melbourne as one of the marquee games of the tournament. After the Kangaroos inflicted a 30–6 defeat of the Kiwis in the opening game, England needed to produce a much better performance. Fans and broadcasters feared a heavy defeat of the English would result in many turning away from the tournament before it really began.

If the Australian media were interested at all in the match, they didn't show it. In his blog for *The Guardian* Andy Wilson lamented the apathy of the local scribes, reporting that England's press conference got pulled at the last minute. A media launch for the next year's State of Origin game to be held in Victoria was considered much more important. In the eyes of the local media, England needed to earn the right to be talked up after years of underachievement against the green and golds. And as New Zealand hired Bennett to instil confidence, the English brought in management consultant Damian Hughes to boost their self-belief.

Melbourne's Docklands Stadium, with retractable roof and unique design, took on the qualities of a big party: 36,297 turned up, including England's 10,000 travelling supporters. By half-time, the atmosphere changed into a wake for the visitors. Australia scored nine tries to one in a 52–4 rout, featuring hat tricks by Billy Slater and Greg Inglis and eight goals by Scott Prince. Slater's ninety-metre run at full pace signified everything the English wanted but didn't have: a real game breaker.

You could hear Love and his team shuffle uncomfortably in the stands. Would this be the death knell for the tournament, just one week after it had begun? Some pleaded for tournament staff to engrave Australia's name on the trophy now, as opposed to wasting time playing unnecessary football matches.

In between times, Ireland, Scotland, Tonga, Fiji and Samoa put in great performances, all progressing beyond the pool stages, with the Fijians reaching the semi-finals.

England improved dramatically against the Kiwis in their final pool game, leading 24–8 at one stage, but New Zealand scored heavily in the second half to win 36–24. A semi-final loomed a week later to see who would face Australia in the final. The Kiwis won an entertaining game 32–22. Halfback Nathan Fien's superior kicking game and a mistake-ridden English side meant the final would be a rematch of the 2000 World Cup finals.

I bought a ticket a few weeks before the final in Brisbane, not really going in with much hope for the Kiwis. Benji Marshall and Fien were playing well, but the visitors still looked outclassed and outgunned on paper.

A raft of torrid storms during the week meant there were genuine concerns about whether the match would go ahead. Brisbane had suffered rain so severe that Suncorp Stadium's ground had flooded three times within a few days. A massive tropical storm was predicted to strike just before the game started. That storm never arrived, yet Brisbane still encountered lighting strikes severe enough to damage part of the venue's roof.

A couple of hours before kick-off, scores of Kiwi supporters packed into public transport. Music blared. Blokes in New Zealand jerseys got out their guitars and sang iconic songs. A large gentleman, who seemed to be the ringleader of a group of supporters, shouted what we were all thinking: 'It's like Auckland in here!' I've been to many Tests involving the Kiwis and the Kangaroos and usually the atmosphere between supporters involves the Aussies gently ribbing their southern cousins. On this occasion – the only time this has happened – the underdogs were giving it back with some witty responses. Call it a quiet confidence or a devil-may-care attitude, but the fans certainly felt different about this one.

Unfortunately, for the statistically minded, there was precious little to support this confidence. Since the 2005 Tri-Nations final, the Kiwis had lost eight straight to Australia. In ten years, they'd only had four wins: one each in 1999 and 2003, and two in 2005. There was seemingly a higher chance of thunder and lightning than a New Zealand victory.

Advance Australia fair

The haka has been the focal point of a few controversies in international rugby league. We've learned how Kiwi forward Mita Moha damaged his hamstring after a particularly vigorous pre-match performance in 1970. Dean Bell also admitted that the Kiwis' poor 1988 World Cup final performance may have resulted from too much haka practice.

Almost twenty years later, at a 2006 Tri-Nations match, the perils of live television caused a trans-Tasman and on-field incident that spilled over into the post-match media. As the New Zealand Internationals lined-up and performed their famous haka the cameras focused on the colourful, giant Kangaroos forward, Willie Mason, and captured Willie mouthing a poorly-timed obscenity in an aside to his teammate. Accusations and insults flew but it was Willie who paid the price on the pitch for inadvertently offending the Kiwis when David Kidwell's accurate shoulder-charge left his mark on Mason's eye socket moments later. The Australians won the ensuing bitter match, but it put much-needed fire into international rugby league.

A particularly heated moment during the Kiwis' haka before the World Cup final. Australia advanced towards New Zealand and both teams almost came into contact during the traditional challenge. Photosport

Two years later, the English tried something similar. They turned their backs on Adam Blair and his Kiwis during their final pool match of the 2008 World Cup, facing each other in a circle instead of facing the challenge head-on. Issac Luke did his absolute best to get his head in their huddle. Yet Ricky Stuart and the Australians had a new, original idea to put the Kiwis off in the biggest game of them all.

Luke and Blair started a particularly emotional haka. The Australians stood in a long line, quite a distance away. Here's where the sporting theatre kicked in. They all linked arms and walked forward, issuing a challenge of their own, slowly reaching the halfway line. The Kiwis advanced too. Would the two sides come to blows? The crowd loved it. So did the Kiwis, who later told newspapers they enjoyed the opposition's tactics.

Lockyer drops the World Cup

Darren Lockyer stood by himself, hands by his side, and addressed his team in the changing room. His coach's focus on encouraging pride in the Australian jersey resonated with the brilliant five-eighth. Lockyer loved every minute of his fifty-nine Tests – from his ill-fated debut that handed the Kiwis a win through to winning Four Nations glory in his last match in 2011 – and took on the role as captain with immense pride. Now, minutes before the World Cup final, he had the honour of giving his troops the final instructions.

When I asked Stuart how he would describe his coaching philosophy, I thought he would talk about man management or tactics. Instead, he laughed sheepishly and told me, 'Ask the players.' As a 'player's coach', he empowered his team to take ownership. Lockyer's words of wisdom embodied this unique approach.

It was all the more poignant considering the Australian captain's struggles that year. The public didn't know it at the time but Lockyer seriously contemplated not playing the 2008 representative season. The toll of so many high-level football matches had wearied him. Bennett revealed in his book *Don't Die with the Music in You* that Lockyer told him of these concerns in a lengthy conversation before the season started. Now, in a World Cup final, his club coach sat in the opposition's box and watched the Broncos skipper kick-off the match.

'We started out of the blocks quickly,' recalled Stuart. 'We had a chance to take a fourteen- or sixteen-point lead early but dropped it over the goal-line.'

Call it divine intervention or plain bad luck, but Lockyer fluffed the grounding. Smith's kick was timed with such perfection that all Lockyer had to do was catch and fall to the turf. Somehow the five-eighth lost control. There were only millimetres in it. No try. Australia had the chance to go up 16–0 and kill the Kiwis off.

The Kiwis were pumped. Jeremy Smith did his best impression of a bowling ball five minutes later, knocking over Anthony Laffranchi, Craig Fitzgibbon and Billy Slater to score New Zealand's first try. More controversy followed, when Benji Marshall's step and weave set up Jerome Ropati to score a second try. Laffranchi had raked the ball out of Marshall's hands, but referee Ashley Klein called play on. After staring down the barrel of a ten-point lead, the Kiwis now were leading by two.

Monaghan's mistake

Australia fought back to lead 16–12 at half-time. But privately the Kiwis felt the momentum was in the balance. Nathan Fien had clearly tried to negate Slater's influence in the first half by kicking low and into the corners, giving him little space to move. The trouble with playing this Australian side was trying to limit the sheer number of their attacking options.

Kangaroo teams always had at least one or two game-breaking players throughout their history; think Churchill, Gasnier, Raper, Stirling, Lewis and Meninga. The 2008 World Cup final team had one of their most potent back-lines ever: fullback Slater, with Greg Inglis and Folau in the centres. Lockyer and Johnathan Thurston controlled play expertly in the halves, while Cameron Smith gave classy service at hooker.

So, how do you stop a team that can attack with so much strike power? Halting the rugby league equivalent of a squadron of F18 fighter jets is a daunting assignment. The New Zealanders had some ideas though. Kearney had watched countless videos of Slater in the lead-up to the final, desperately trying to find a chink to exploit. Slater tended to set up on the left-hand side in defence if there was a right-footed kicker (like Benji Marshall on this occasion). So, why not try the opposite side where Slater couldn't reach?

The plan would be as follows: Fien would kick for fullback Lance Hohaia, who would run parallel alongside him. With just ten minutes left and the Kiwis leading by two points, Fien kicked ahead. He recalls what happened next:

> We shifted the play from left to right, which didn't allow Slater to be in the frame [to attack the ball]. Lance ran up on my inside and followed the kick through. It took a wicked bounce, bouncing much more than Joel Monaghan expected it to. He made a grab at Lance before he could get to the ball. We all thought it would be a penalty.

Video referee Steve Ganson had six or seven looks at the replay. Hohaia was onside and timed his run perfectly. Monaghan touched the ball as it bounced up awkwardly, right into Hohaia's path. Monaghan had a vital decision to make. Would he watch Hohaia score the winning try or stop him? The Kangaroos winger couldn't help himself and grabbed New Zealand's number 1 around his shoulders, preventing him from getting a fair go at the football. Up in the commentary box, Phil Gould was adamant it should be a penalty try, whereas Peter Stirling and Ray Warren needed more convincing. After a good few minutes of agony for everyone on the ground, the big green sign flashed on the screen: PENALTY TRY.

The crowd screamed simultaneously with delight and disbelief. I sat with a big contingent of English supporters who had stayed to watch the final. They suddenly became very animated too, excited by New Zealand's now strong chances of victory.

Defending like demons

The Kangaroos had a long history of winning Test matches when all looked lost. Kearney was there when the Kiwis' defence crumbled in the previous World Cup final. He watched as a fan seven years later as Australia and Great Britain notched up wins of 58-0 and 44-0 during the end-of-year Tests. Now, as Kiwis coach, he made sure his players approached defence differently. It was about attitude, discipline and execution. The result would culminate in a great team play that left Kearney feeling very proud.

From a scrum, Australia moved the ball out to bearded winger David Williams, who starting running close to the touch-line. The Kiwis smelled an opportunity to show their coach just how committed they were. Like a pack of lions charging a helpless gazelle, five Kiwi players dragged the shell-shocked Australian and dumped him over the touch-line, his head bouncing off the damp turf like a spring. Jeremy Smith pumped his fists in delight, waving his hands and screaming at the Australian players. It was a crucial play and he knew it.

Ray Haffenden also knew the importance of that moment. The New Zealand Rugby League delegate had wandered down from his corporate box to take in the atmosphere and noticed Darren Lockyer standing by himself. Never rattled and always a picture of calm, the Kangaroos skipper looked like a man without ideas. Haffenden remembered: 'Lockyer didn't look happy. His hands were by his side. He had that look as if to say, "What do we do next?"'

Lockyer couldn't prevent the Kiwis bundling Williams into touch. The winger lay there for about a minute. He was dazed and confused, as were the rest of the Kangaroos. The momentum was starting to turn even more in the visitors' direction, courtesy of an error that would be talked about for years to come.

A Slater speculator

Billy Slater's high-risk play near the end of the World Cup final had commentators, fans and media pundits declaring it a crime equal to the Great Train Robbery. Why would the brilliant fullback try such a low percentage option with the game in the balance? What was going through his mind?

It shouldn't have come as a complete surprise for observers who had followed Slater's career closely. He attacked all the time, took risks and backed his ability. Unfortunately for the fullback, his gamble didn't pay off this time.

Slater had celebrated a phenomenal individual year. He had won basically every award available in 2008: Dally M Fullback of the Year, Rugby League Week Player of the Year, Rugby League International Federation Fullback of the Year and, the grandest of all for an international footballer, the Golden Boot – the award for the world's best player. He'd lit up State of Origin in his second match, scoring a freakish try. He'd also made his Test match debut. The rugby league world was in love with the country lad. The World Cup was his chance to showcase his unique brand of fearless football to a massive television audience.

As a youngster in Innisfail, far north Queensland, Slater's first love wasn't rugby league: it was horses. He'd competed in show jumping and equestrian events for many years, only stopping when rugby league came knocking quite by chance. The local rugby league team was short of players one day and asked Slater to have a go. He enjoyed it and continued to thrive. Then at sixteen, Slater faced the biggest decision in his young life. He'd managed to crack the town's representative rugby league team, but he was also offered a chance to work for esteemed racehorse trainer Gai Waterhouse. He chose the latter.

Waterhouse taught the young apprentice about discipline, dedication and hard work. Slater's six-month stint involved rising at 2.30am every day, seven days a week, to feed and walk the horses, as well as sweeping out the stables. The experience would also be great for his rugby league. Apart from what he learned from Waterhouse, he went through a physical transformation, from skinny teenager to muscled young man. All the stable duties served as a kind of outdoor gym. After being offered a trial by the Melbourne Storm, he had an outstanding few years at NRL level before impressing at Origin and Test level.

Few could match Slater's acceleration in attack. But often overlooked was his ball-playing ability. Throughout the 2008 tournament, he created and set up tries galore, a reason he was awarded the Player of the Tournament. Like the horses he cared for as a teenager, Slater had seemingly reached his peak during the biggest race of all.

Benji Marshall punted downfield, hoping to find space. But Slater was too fast and brilliantly caught the football on his fingertips. The fullback paused to look at the assignment in front of him. Two men were chasing down the left flank: Manu Vatuvei and Jerome Ropati. Vatuvei, at 1.89 metres and 112 kilograms, made a strong case for being one of the biggest men in rugby league at the time. During the Melbourne Storm's match against the New Zealand Warriors earlier in the year, Slater had faced the same situation as he did now. He'd managed to take on Vatuvei and beat him for pace on the outside.

Slater decided to try the same tactic. He would back his pace against the bigger man again. After all, his team was down 20–22 and needed some of his magic. Slater approached the big winger and stepped off his left foot, but Vatuvei managed to push the fullback towards the side-line. Slater could either take the ball into touch or try and keep it in play, so he flung the ball in-field, hoping to find someone in a Kangaroos jersey. Marshall, who had followed through his kick, couldn't believe his eyes as the ball bounced in front of him. He picked it up and scored in the corner. His teammates all ran over for a hug in celebration.

During the lead-up to the World Cup final of 2013, journalists kept asking him whether he regretted the error. A relaxed Slater simply replied his self-belief never waivered and, although he made a mistake, it didn't change anything about his approach to the game. He would make amends by scoring two tries and helping the Kangaroos to a big victory.

Australia trailed by eight points with fifteen minutes to go. Along with Slater, they could employ Inglis, Thurston, Lockyer, Folau and Smith to put in an all-out assault on the Kiwis' defence.

One last chance

Darren Lockyer was named Man of the Match, but Jeremy Smith could have easily claimed it for the Kiwis with an act of desperation. An elusive Thurston dummied and raced through a big gap, with New Zealand players falling over to stop him. Smith managed to trip Thurston up with a last-ditch ankle-tap. Australia's hopes were dashed as their halfback tumbled over.

Darren Lockyer: so many times he got Australia out of trouble but even his two tries (and a man-of-the-match performance) wasn't enough in the final. RLPhotos.com

Wayne Bennett's words of self-belief echoed through the minds of the men in black. Stephen Kearney's discipline and preparation ensured they would focus until the end. Adam Blair had the last say as he scooped up a loose ball to score, ensuring there wouldn't be any comeback from the Kangaroos this time. The Kiwis had done the unthinkable.

No regrets

'The black and white ball is underway,' commentator Ray Warren summed up the pandemonium on the field as referee Klein called for full-time.

A proud New Zealand media shared their joy too, gushing with praise across talkback radio, television and print media. Kiwis went from vanquished to victors in less than a year. Kearney and Bennett's collective coaching talents were undeniably vital, however the 'brotherhood' within the camp also played a huge part. The players clearly wanted to play for each other and go where no other Kiwi team had gone before.

The night became a triumph for Benji Marshall. His famous 'flick-pass' during the 2005 NRL grand final established his early legacy, but after a number of shoulder injuries he had thoughts of giving the game away. As he recounted in his autobiography, a game of touch football with his older cousins taught him how to tough things out. Now, with a winner's medal around his neck, all the pain and hours of rehab seemed worth it.

How do you quantify the impact of winning a World Cup for the first time? Maybe it was the unseen, like the big contingent of fans that stayed at the ground for hours after the game, soaking up the enormity of the moment. Grown men were reduced to tears. Strangers hugged each other as I walked out of Suncorp Stadium that night. Veteran *New Zealand Herald* sports writer Dylan Cleaver summed up his excitement the next day by proclaiming, 'The Kiwis are the World Champions!' four times in his match report. Sports journalists, it seemed, also got unashamedly giddy. Maybe, like the general public, they simply couldn't believe that New Zealand had managed to win against all odds.

Scoreboard: **New Zealand 34** (Lance Hohaia 2, Jeremy Smith, Jerome Ropati, Benji Marshall, Adam Blair tries; Issac Luke 3, Marshall 2 goals) defeated **Australia 20** (Darren Lockyer 2, Greg Inglis, David Williams tries; Johnathan Thurston 2 goals). Crowd: 50,509.

Match 10, 2013

THE EPIC TO LAST A LIFETIME

England v. New Zealand

23 November 2013
Wembley Stadium, London, England
World Cup semi-final

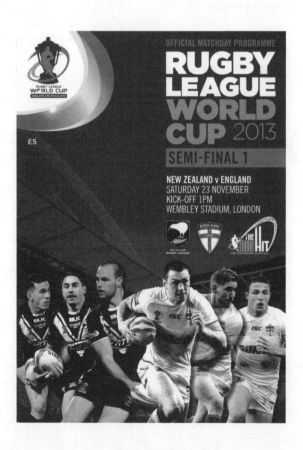

ENGLAND	NEW ZEALAND
1. Sam Tomkins	1. Kevin Locke
2. Josh Charnley	2. Roger Tuivasa-Sheck
3. Kallum Watkins	3. Dean Whare
4. Leroy Cudjoe	4. Bryson Goodwin
5. Ryan Hall	5. Jason Nightingale
6. Gareth Widdop	6. Kieran Foran
7. Kevin Sinfield (captain)	7. Shaun Johnson
8. James Graham	8. Jared Waerea-Hargreaves
9. James Roby	9. Issac Luke
10. Sam Burgess	10. Jesse Bromwich
11. Brett Ferres	13. Simon Mannering (captain)
12. Ben Westwood	12. Sonny Bill Williams
13. Sean O'Loughlin	17. Elijah Taylor
Interchange:	Interchange:
14. Rob Burrow	14. Frank-Paul Nu'uausala
15. George Burgess	15. Sam Kasiano
16. Chris Hill	16. Ben Matulino
17. Carl Ablett	17. Alex Glenn
Coach: Steve McNamara	Coach: Stephen Kearney

Referee: Ben Cummins

As the clock ticked over to 4.30 in the morning New Zealand time, most Kiwi fans had either gone to bed or were contemplating the ultimate double-whammy: a poor night's sleep and the bitter resentment of defeat. Meanwhile, at a noisy Wembley Stadium in London, an ocean of English supporters decked out in white and red were basking in what would be a gutsy, tough win against the reigning world champions. There is something delicious about being in the stands when your team wins, particularly in a gruelling match like this. Within a few minutes, beers would be drunk, glasses raised and ill-fated promises made. You also felt that *Get Lucky, Blurred Lines* or *Roar,* plus the other hits of 2013 would blast from sound systems everywhere. All of these song titles would be appropriate to this match when it was over.

'The Big Hit' marketing campaign, featuring the two semi-finals back-to-back, was targeted to capture the London and southeast England market. As the capital bathed in the success of hosting the Olympic Games a year earlier, the city had got a taste of large sporting events and liked it. This time around, the tournament organisers were hopeful of putting on an exciting spectacle for those perhaps new to the code. Thankfully, England's superb match against New Zealand ensured the marketing team made good on their promises.

World class

World Cup general manager Sally Bolton had seen first-hand the highs and lows of previous tournament incarnations going back as far as 1995. She had been involved in a mixture of marketing, events and project management roles with the Rugby Football League and latterly the Rugby League International Federation, so she was well positioned to take the 2013 World Cup into a new level of excellence alongside tournament director Nigel Wood.

She heeded the lessons of 2000's tournament, which she believed the tournament organisers had tried to expand too much before the sport was ready. Eighteen months wasn't enough time to plan for such a large operation. So, the 2013 World Cup tournament team put in four years' worth of planning. Bolton had a clear vision of what she wanted to achieve this time around.

> In the early period, we had a strong sense of needing to grow the sport internationally. How you do this in the context of a tournament is an ongoing debate, but we felt it was about balancing quality with a good spread of nations to demonstrate rugby league was actually growing.

There was one key difference with her strategy that was brand new in UK sporting parlance: allowing cities to bid for matches. It doesn't sound profound, but it revolutionised the whole feeling of the World Cup. Rugby league hotbeds like Hull and Wigan had to put up meaningful business cases about why they should host important matches.

On the back of the 2012 Olympics, there was a strong sense in the UK that sporting events could be used to get more communities involved. For this World Cup, cities really were strongly engaged in the whole process, and used tournaments to drive their own agendas, building community ownership of the teams as well as selling tickets.

One of the winners in this competitive approach was Rochdale. The town and its rugby league team, the Rochdale Hornets, campaigned to host the Fiji versus Ireland pool match on the strength of their long and deep connection with Fijians. After the Hornets signed two Fijian rugby union stars in 1961 – Orisi Dawai and Joe Levula – many more came to Rochdale. The city found support in many different quarters: the BBC did a recording prior to the game, local TV and radio did stories about the Hornets, and the Fijian team sang a hymn in the town hall – all contributing to a sense of strong community. After ten months of campaigning it all paid off: a crowd of just over 8,000 fans turned out to see Fiji defeat Ireland 32–14. Tournament staff had predicted closer to 1,000 – if they were lucky.

The decision to include fourteen teams (up from ten the previous tournament) once again raised fears about early mismatches, but there was a definite strategy behind getting this right from the opening match that differed from previous events. Wood explained:

> In constructing the tournament, particular attention
> was given to insuring that nations of similar ability were
> pooled and that these matches were placed at venues
> that best suited such fixtures. Great attention was placed
> on the opening round of fixtures to ensure that the
> tournament got away to a really vibrant and enthralling

start that would then roll forward to the rest of the
group fixtures.

Thankfully, Australia versus England and Samoa's big
comeback against New Zealand on the opening weekend
had a great flow-on effect for the rest of the matches. France's
last-gasp win against Papua New Guinea was another real
highlight. Just like in 2008, the lesser league nations could
call upon a host of established NRL and Super League stars.
Petero Civoniceva captained Fiji, Anthony Minichello led
the Italians and the likes of Tonga, Samoa, Scotland and
Wales all had enough big names to lure the crowds.

The 2013 tournament also promised to be by far the most
ambitious yet: Wood wanted all venues to have a minimum of
75 per cent spectator occupancy. This would take some doing,
even considering the strongly performed 2008 World Cup.

A carnival atmosphere

Premier Sports and the BBC shared the broadcasting rights
in England, with Sky Sport, Setanta Sport, 7mate and beIN
Sport beaming coverage to New Zealand, Ireland, Australia
and France. The television figures for the past two World
Cups were pretty good, so there was a general sense that the
2013 tournament would take this success to new dimensions.
It did, with 18.8 million television viewers tuning in. Neal
Coupland, who ran the media for the RFL in 2000, was
now the Executive Producer for Premier Sport's coverage
and had a unique take on what he wanted to give to his
network's passionate subscribers.

Coupland sought out long-time rugby league broadcaster Andrew Voss to anchor his coverage. With a relaxed, fun and down-to-earth style of calling matches, Voss became the voice of the tournament. His brief was simple: engage with the fans, relax and enjoy himself. He certainly did all three, encapsulated by this example. Before the Kiwis' match against Samoa in Warrington, Voss arrived very early to start his preparation. A few hours afterwards, not long until game time, he told his colleagues he was going for a walk. Coupland thought he might have gone to the pub. He did, but not for a booze-up.

It turns out he had been to the Rodney Arms to sample a pork roll and chat with the locals. He returned in time to start the game. During the commentary, he surprisingly mentioned about his food and pub journey earlier that day. The fans loved it and suddenly Warrington was abuzz with suggestions about where to go for food, rolls and pubs. It became a social media party. Voss's bright and lively commentating captured the carnival atmosphere of the World Cup perfectly. Twitter continued to pay tribute to Voss's performances and food adventures a couple of years later.

Selection dramas

There was one piece of the World Cup puzzle that dominated headlines before and during the event: whether Sonny Bill Williams, a rugby league superstar turned World Cup-winning All Black, would be available to play. If he was fit, it was surely a no-brainer; he had to play. The deluge of rumours and coverage devoted to Williams was more appropriate to *The Australian Women's Weekly* or *The Sun* than the national newspapers. But the man nicknamed SBW had that much star power in 2013 that he could have created his own solar system.

Williams had played seven Tests in his initial NRL career between 2004 and 2008. In one of sport's ironies, he won titles, tournaments and awards soon after defecting to rugby union. But his international rugby league career was very unremarkable; he'd never been on the winning side in a Test match.

After a long, bruising year back in the NRL, where opposition defenders seemed to deliberately target him as if he carried a bounty, Williams became more and more non-committal about his future plans. Talkback radio lines ran hot on whether either code's most exciting player would join the Kiwis in their World Cup bid.

Let's go forward to Tuesday, 8 October and World Cup squad naming day. Stephen Kearney read out his team. Williams wasn't in it; he'd decided to skip the tournament and have a break instead. He'd sent this tweet (later deleted) the previous night:

> Wishing the kiwis all the best in their title defence, having my first break since 2008. Looking forward to spending time with fam n friends
> – Sonny Bill Williams (@SonnyBWilliams) October 7, 2013

The Kiwis moved on with their preparations. They already had enviable depth in the second-row position, with the likes of Simon Mannering, Elijah Taylor, Alex Glenn and Frank Pritchard able to cover the spot. Kearney also delighted in welcoming twenty-one-year-old Tohu Harris into international football for the first time. The 1.95-metre, 108-kilogram forward had only made his first-grade debut that year for the Melbourne Storm. He possessed good ball-handling skills to go with his athletic frame and had a big future ahead of him. It was a lovely story and one that got New Zealand's campaign off to a bright, heart-warming start. Harris's parents, Paul and Dale, quickly booked UK-bound flights to see their son play.

Everything changed twenty-four hours later.

Williams had a sudden change of heart and decided to make himself available for selection. After time to reflect, he didn't want to leave the game with any regrets. A chance to help the Kiwis in their World Cup bid was back on the agenda.

All well and good for Williams, but it put Kearney in a very awkward situation: he would have to drop someone to accommodate him. He chose Harris. All that goodwill had disappeared in a flash – or in this case a Tweet – and Harris's disappointed parents cancelled their tickets. Williams once again took to Twitter to express his feelings (it was later deleted also):

> I'm really sorry about the Tohu situation it was never my intention I just followed my heart, now i promise ill play with all of it. #Kiwis
>
> – Sonny Bill Williams (@SonnyBWilliams) October 9, 2013

Williams' about-turn meant he received vitriol from rugby league fans in both Australia and New Zealand. Many felt betrayed not just by Williams, but also by Kearney and the New Zealand Rugby League, whom they felt were weak by accommodating one player's wishes ahead of the team cause. Kiwis' selector Richie Barnett at the time felt Williams disrespected the rest of the squad with his actions, but he stood by his vote to choose him. It's professional sport after all. A couple of years later, Barnett had modified his position slightly.

> It was a group decision [to select Williams]. I really felt
> for Tohu Harris – he is an amazing person and player –
> but those feelings didn't change the decision though.
> Over time you learn from your experiences … and
> looking back, it compromised our values as a team.

The New Zealand media were split over the whole saga. Chris Rattue didn't hold back in his column for the *New Zealand Herald*, declaring it a day of shame for NZ rugby league. Following Williams's last-minute inclusion he felt the team didn't stand for anything worthwhile any more. Conversely, his colleague Michael Brown was adamant that Williams had to be included and the selectors were duty-bound to choose the best squad. New Zealand rugby league and the Kiwis lost a few fans that day, yet the Rugby League World Cup organisers were rubbing their hands together with glee.

The Kiwis' odds of winning the event shortened dramatically from $6 to $4.25 at the TAB after SBW's inclusion. During the tournament's media launch, Williams was the big focus and became the face of the tournament overnight. English sports fans took to social media to express their excitement in watching the giant second-row forward on their shores. Neal Coupland told me how much Williams added to the commercial and broadcasting figures once he joined the squad:

> SBW's inclusion made such a difference. The media in the UK went ballistic and ticket sales went through the roof. The Warrington [NZ v Samoa] game got sold out in a couple of days and it had a positive knock-on effect for other games, really creating fantastic momentum. Sonny Bill Williams also was the number one ranked topic in our broadcasting figures.

Williams went on to star in the All Blacks' 2015 World Cup win and gained himself universal respect for his achievements and humility. But for a few weeks in October and November 2013, whether you thought he was arrogant, selfish or very talented, something else rang true: Williams's involvement made that year's Rugby League World Cup much more interesting viewing.

Two-team mentality

Steve McNamara had served a solid apprenticeship at domestic and international levels before taking over the England head-coaching role in 2010. He played close to 300 games in the Super League for Bradford, Hull, Wakefield and Huddersfield as a goal-kicking loose forward, and gained a handful of caps for Great Britain.

Passionate, loyal and honest, his 2008 World Cup experience as England assistant really shaped his coaching career. The country's poor performances were dragged down even further when UK media outlets like the BBC reported rumours of a split between Leeds and St Helens, the two super-clubs. McNamara told the BBC's Angela Powers on *Super League Superstars* that it wasn't a pleasant time in his career, but it also wasn't quite as bad as some sections of the media made it out to be:

> There was a lot of talk about St Helens and Leeds but nothing was quite as bad as everybody said. There was no real animosity between the players within the group but they weren't the best of friends. That was the circumstances at the time, in terms of the number of times the England team could get together and what they could achieve.

Their failure — a win against Papua New Guinea was their only success — led to a complete overhaul of the England program after a review by the Rugby Football League. They announced a seven-point plan to improve the Test side's performance. This centred on the squad of twenty-five to thirty players meeting four times a year, giving the team more chances to train together. An RFL-generated report led by executive director Richard Lewis revealed that the players felt they could have had more time for bonding, training together and simply getting to know each other. Lewis also poured cold water on the team split rumours, saying there was no evidence it impacted the performance of the team. Make your own mind up about what happened.

After being elevated to the England head coach role in 2010, McNamara took everything he'd learned and set about instilling a long-lasting sense of team unity.

It centred on what he coined a 'two-club' philosophy. England players would represent both their club and country throughout a season. Key players like Kevin Sinfield and Sam Tomkins spoke positively in public about the idea, and England's results steadily improved. They reached the finals of the 2009 and 2011 Four Nations, each time knocking off New Zealand but failing to beat Australia. Along with the main team, the RFL formed an England 'A' side and improved access to sports science as well as better training facilities.

As the Kiwis geared up to take on Samoa in the opening match, England would face Australia at the Millennium Stadium in Cardiff. After an intensive training camp in Potchefstroom, South Africa, England's campaign caught fire before it started. They suffered an embarrassing pre-tournament defeat to lowly ranked Italy. Even though it wasn't considered a full Test match, the team weren't happy with their performance and it led to a squad breach of discipline. Forward Gareth Hock was sensationally dropped from the World Cup squad for breaking the team alcohol ban. Hock later claimed that 'six or seven' were out drinking too.

McNamara insisted he would focus on his team's preparation and it wouldn't be affected. In a testy press conference, the media never received an answer about why key forward James Graham wasn't selected to play Australia.

A good crowd of more than 45,000 turned out to watch a vibrant opening ceremony, as well as a pretty strong performance by the home side. Australia finished well and executed better at the end, winning 28–20. England had managed to score the most points against Australia of any team since the Kiwis' 20–34 loss in 2010. But the Kangaroos eased their way to victory with superior possession and territory. England were good, but not good enough.

Shock the World

The USA rugby league team was undoubtedly the tournament's feel-good story. Known as the 'Tomahawks', the side were 1,000–1 outsiders before the tournament started. Their achievements over the next few weeks inspired a popular band to pen a song in their honour, *The New York Times* to write a feature article and sponsors to sign. This story has three main characters: David Niu, Steve Johnson and Terry Matterson, all contributing in many different ways.

In 1996, Niu, a former first-grade player with St George, took action to plan a domestic rugby league competition in America. After arriving in the States from Australia three years earlier, he organised an American team to the World Sevens and put together an annual fixture against Ireland at RFK Stadium, Washington D.C. This was all exciting and he saw potential in the sport, but now he wanted to see it grow organically. So, he started a competition one Friday night in a local school in Philadelphia, with fifteen jerseys he'd 'found from somewhere'. Fifteen players took on each other in a seven-a-side game. It grew from there. Thirty people turned out the following week. From 1996 to 1998, the USA played an annual game against Canada. It grew to become the American National Rugby League and featured twelve teams. Niu reflected on rugby league in America at that time:

> I felt rugby league was closely related to American football, with both moving the ball down the field. It was a relatable sport. I set about creating a plan and building some teams. Rugby league and union were on an equal footing at the time, with league having a niche in the east coast. We took on touring teams, including club and English amateur sides, and the sport grew and grew.

The USA took part in the 1995 Emerging Nations World Cup, but missed out on qualifying for the full World Cup in 2000. The team then spent the next decade in limbo, as they continued to host touring sides (the 2004 match against Australia was a highlight of that period) but missed out on getting to the 2008 event.

Niu's long-term goal was always to qualify for the 2013 World Cup. He wanted Americans to get excited about rugby league and watch their side play on the world stage. Queensland lawyer and rugby league fan Steve Johnson set out to identify eligible professional players as well as develop the domestic group. With Matthew Elliott as coach (with more than a decade's experience in the Super League and NRL), excitement continued to build in the group.

They faced Jamaica and South Africa in 2011 in the Atlantic region's World Cup qualifying tournament. Johnson remembers how he and Niu spent the night before their match against Jamaica having to put grass over the baseball diamond on Campbell's Field, New Jersey. It seemed the island team didn't want to play on sand – quite ironic, don't you think? The Tomahawks defeated both teams by 40–4 to qualify for the World Cup in eleventh spot. It wasn't the end of it, though, as they had to prove to the Rugby League International Federation that they would be fairly competitive. How do you go about doing that?

Both men continued to work hard to assemble a competitive squad. They brought a number of players from the USA to Australia, helping them become better players and assigning them to different clubs. By mid-2013, the trouble started. Elliott decided to resign from the role after accepting a new job with the New Zealand Warriors, to take part in their upcoming season. Brian Smith, another NRL veteran coach, joined as his replacement but then left right in the middle of the World Cup to return for his son's surprise wedding. Finally, Terry Matterson accepted the role and stayed. He was able to bring the team together nicely and quickly, leaning on the USA's small pool of seasoned NRL stars.

Whereas other nations had the luxury of spending a few weeks in pre-season camps, the majority of the USA team met for the first time two weeks ahead of their first match. It was highly unusual, but the Tomahawks' World Cup squad got to know each other at Heathrow Airport at the end of their flight across the world, rather than in the training paddocks. Still, there was optimism. Parramatta five-eighth Joseph Paulo skippered the team, Matt Petersen held a wing spot and Clint Newton led the way at prop. The others were a talented bunch who bought into Matterson's teachings. He brought Curtis Cunz, their most capped international, and a famous NFL college footballer to speak about the pride in representing the USA.

The Tomahawk players didn't get paid (a small allowance from the tournament organisers notwithstanding). As Johnson reflected with much humour, the whole campaign was funded through his American Express credit card. Despite this, the squad had a great attitude towards their time together, and it showed on the field. Their first assignment was against the Cook Islands, their best chance of a win.

It was a tight tussle for the whole match. Moments of inspiration peppered the Tomahawks' performance, including Paulo's charge-down just after half-time, which led to his try, along with Craig Priestly's brilliant catch off a high bomb to score the match-winner. The USA's 32–20 win was a great start.

Then, it was on to Wales, a much bigger challenge. But skipper Paulo was immense once again. He scored a try, set up more for his colleagues and kicked well. The Welsh were poor early, and the visitors kept attacking through their outside backs, setting up a superb 24–16 victory.

No-one gave the USA any hope. How's this: the RLIF had pre-booked their flights to be after their final pool match, expecting a quick exit. But the US, an unbeaten side, had to rearrange everything. For a while, they had no accommodation booked or a way home. On the week of their final pool match against Scotland, Niu made a call to a famous friend: Anthony Field, creator and lead singer of The Wiggles. I asked Field what motivated him to write a song about the team.

> David sent me a tweet and asked if I could come up with
> a theme song for the Tomahawks. They were certainly
> the underdogs and I liked the whole idea of it. They
> were the fairy-tale team. David came up with the great
> slogan, 'Shock the World', because that's what he wanted
> the team to do.

Shock the World became an instant hit, attracting more than 500,000 views on YouTube within a few days, and it was even played at the grounds in England. More press continued, including a feature story in *The New York Times*, the first time the national team got such widespread exposure.

A quarter final against Australia was always going to stretch a team of mostly amateur footballers. Even so, the Tomahawks put in a big-hearted performance, holding the Kangaroos out for big parts of the game before a clump of tries ended their maiden World Cup journey.

In a trip of many highlights, Johnson's fondest memory came after their World Cup warm-up win against France.

> I remember standing in France, after we had beaten
> them 22–18, and both David [in Philadelphia] and I

were crying on the phone. David had put in so much work over the years as well as those who had worn the Tomahawk jersey. David had taken the very rocks people threw at him [he got a lot of criticism for not selecting all domestic players] and turned it into something wonderful. We'd just beaten France, something that New Zealand and Australia haven't done in different times. That moment sticks in my mind. There we were, I was in France and he was in Philadelphia, both just crying with emotion.

This emotion and goodwill ended after their tournament finished. Niu resigned from his role as the ANRL CEO due to political faction-fighting. In his words, 'a couple of guys with different agendas undid fifteen years of work' by forming a breakaway league. Rugby league in America needs clear thinking and positive action if they want to get back to their glory days of that World Cup.

Points to prove

England and New Zealand both had cause to be jittery on the eve of their semi-final. In a curious quirk, both sides had contested Four Nations finals since the 2008 World Cup – but never against each other. Australia had played in each one. As the Kangaroos had blazed their way in the pool and quarter-final stages, scoring a combined total of 172 for, 22 against, the two semi-finalists had put in some patchy performances. Both were yet to put in a complete one and they knew it.

Kevin Sinfield remarked that this match would be the biggest game of his and his side's careers. A great deal of steel seemed to wrap around Sinfield and his coach as they spoke on the eve of the match, knowing that their respective Test careers could conceivably be over within a few hours. Both also did their best to squash what the media tried to paint as disharmony in the camp, when young fullback Zak Hardaker was expelled from the squad just before England's final pool match against Fiji for an undisclosed reason.

Most importantly, if the Lions could beat the Kiwis, it would mean a rare chance to play a World Cup final at home. The English camp was quietly confident.

By the same token, Kearney and his Kiwis were slightly on edge. The coach admitted how strong their opponents had become over recent years and reflected on New Zealand's poor record in England – their last win against a British side was in 2005 – that 'burned inside' him and many of his players. It was a record they were keen to improve. But, in true, low-key Kearney style, he wanted to take things one game at a time.

McNamara made one key change to his starting line-up, bringing in Gareth Widdop and dropping Rangi Chase. The Kiwis brought in Jason Nightingale for an injured Manu Vatuvei and reshuffled their forward pack.

Band of brothers

When all four Burgess brothers – Sam, Tom, George and Luke – were named in the South Sydney Rabbitohs side to face Wests Tigers in April 2013, it marked a historic moment in rugby league. It was only the second time in 103 years that four brothers had appeared in a first-grade game.

Although Luke was the eldest, Sam had paved a path for his siblings to follow when he joined South Sydney from Bradford in 2010, swapping snow for sunshine. Already a capped international player, his whole-hearted attitude and impact play caught the eye of Russell Crowe, who, as the Rabbitoh's part-owner, wanted to take his beloved club back to the glory days of the previous decade. Crowe saw something special in the young firebrand. Sam had confidence in spades and didn't seem to get overawed by big occasions; on Test debut, he put in a huge shoulder-charge tackle on Kiwi behemoth Fuifui Moimoi. What an entrance.

Crowe also saw value in bringing Sam's brothers over to Sydney too, not just to keep him company, but also to instil a real sense of brotherhood to the club. Nothing beats blood connections.

The England coaching set-up decided to elevate George and Thomas to the international arena for the first time, meaning they became the first trio of brothers to play in an England rugby league side. All played in the opening match against Australia, with George scoring a try. But spare a thought for Luke, the eldest, who didn't get the World Cup call-up.

As the semi-final got underway, Sam started the match at prop, with George on the bench. The older brother's battle with Sonny Bill Williams got the crowd up in their seats as the two giants clashed in defence or in attack. Williams struggled for any real time to assert his dominance as he frequently encountered a host of English jumpers ready to stop him. Sam continued to hunt around the ruck, looking for new ways to impose himself on the match and the opposition.

He told viewers in his *Slammin' Sam* documentary that as a youngster, he always wanted to be the best player in every game he played. He wanted to do something special or significant. This continued push for excellence throughout his career extended to the semi-final, where he was later voted Man of the Match. Among the two biggest packs in world rugby league, Burgess seemed a foot taller that day. He was immense.

Burgess made his mark twice in the Kiwis' first use of the football. On tackle one, he clattered into New Zealand's Jared Waerea-Hargreaves on the first tackle with Graham's help, then joined O'Loughlin in a four-man tackle on Williams on the third tackle. He was like an angry bear, sniffing out chances to get an advantage to his team.

He sparkled in attack too, choosing the right moment to burst through Shaun Johnson's tackle and offloading to his skipper to score the first try of the game after a tense opening seventeen minutes. A Sinfield penalty pushed the home side to a handy 8–0 a few minutes later.

The Kiwis attack was in good working order. After all, they had scored thirty-four tries in four games coming into the match, so they shouldn't have felt too concerned. Their first try would be a certified 'Wembley moment', one that will stand as one of the greatest tries scored at the venue.

Whare flick

Benji Marshall's audacious 'flick-pass' for the Wests Tigers during the 2005 NRL grand final had people rubbing their eyes in disbelief. Eight years later, New Zealand centre Dean Whare conjured a play that trumped even his fellow countryman. Let's call it the 'mid-air flick'.

Kieran Foran began with a set cross-field kick for Nightingale, right in the corner of the left-hand touch-line. Now, here's where the crowd saw some great skill. After Nightingale tipped it back in play, the New Zealanders managed to keep the ball alive, getting it to Issac Luke in mid-field. He fired a long, loopy pass that missed all his teammates and bounced dangerously into touch. Here's where the magic happened.

The ball had no right to stay in the field of play. It bounced along merrily, heading for the touch-line. But

Sam Burgess put England ahead by 18–14 with eight minutes to go.
RLPhotos.com

the best players of any sport seem to have a little bit more time than lesser players. Darren Lockyer had it. So did Dan Carter. Whare might not reach their heights, but he showed us all how gifted he was right at this moment. He attacked the ball without fear of footing it out. In one motion, while his feet were mid-stride and in the air, he caught the football and transferred it back to a surprised Roger Tuivasa-Sheck who was watching in support. His timing needed to be perfect. It was.

Whare said it was a part of his game he had worked on (the pass, not necessarily pulling off near-miracle plays) and modestly felt he was lucky to get it away.

With the conversion and a late penalty goal by Johnson, the teams went into half-time at 8–8. The Kiwis were hanging in there despite the home side's dominance across the park.

It was absorbing. Both sides traded tries and penalties, finding space and holes out wide. For much of the second half, it was simply Burgess, Graham, Ferres, Westwood and O'Loughlin running at Waerea-Hargreaves, Bromwich, Mannering and Williams. Rinse and repeat.

The crowd, which reached almost 70,000 that afternoon, remained tense. Sure, they crowed and roared whenever the home side found a gap or dished out a particularly bone-crunching hit. But they really only started to find their voice when Sam Burgess burst through a gap on his own thirty-metre line.

Sinfield was again the creator, drawing in Williams and Johnson before slipping a deft pass to a bulldozing Burgess.

The most amazing thing about his run is that you felt like he was going to score as soon as he got the ball. He oozed confidence. Nothing made you feel like he was going to come up short as he sprinted into space, stepped around an almost redundant Kevin Locke at fullback and crashed over for a try. England now led. They celebrated like they had won. Perhaps it was the euphoria produced by such a powerful individual try.

The Kiwis started to panic. The gap was four, but with a roaring crowd screaming for the men from the north, it became more like fourteen. Luke kicked the restart out on the full, meaning a penalty. Johnson tried a chip and chase – a high-risk option at the best of times – but Widdop recovered it. Locke threw a wild pass that sailed into touch with five minutes left. The crowd burst into a loud chant: 'England! England! England!' Finally, all those British rugby league fans were going to get what they had craved since 1995: a World Cup final with their team in it.

Magic Johnson

England's fans were to be denied in the cruellest of scenarios. Shaun Johnson stepped, weaved and skipped through to reduce the majority of Wembley to tears. It seemed like a mighty display of confidence and skill under the most intense of situations. But Paul, his father, knew this moment was coming his son's whole life. He had been stepping and running ever since his first day of rugby league.

At twelve months, young Shaun was able to drop-kick a league ball. At just two-years-old he was running 'effortlessly around the paddock' with his local club's under-twelve team. Say it again slowly. A two-year-old infant playing on the same field as kids about to be teenagers. It gets better. Most kids' first utterances are 'Mum', 'Dad' or something else family orientated. Johnson's first word was 'ball'.

Even at a young age, he was very organised, energetic and loved the outdoors. Here's a statistic that makes your head spin. While playing for the Hibiscus Coast Raiders' under-six side, he scored an incredible sixty-three tries in one season. As Paul reflected, he didn't like passing in his earlier years.

With a mixture of natural ability and a burning desire to play the game, Shaun seemed destined for greatness at a very young age. Did his father have any inkling his son was going to play professional sport?

'There was no doubt in my mind he would be a professional rugby league player. From the age of five onwards, I would tell him that he would one day play for the New Zealand Warriors and the Kiwis.'

With his father giving him confidence, coaches who encouraged expression of talent and a good support group around him, Shaun continued to thrive on the sporting field. Apart from league, he played touch rugby (making New Zealand's under-seventeen and under-nineteen squads), rugby union, basketball, hockey and even Australian Rules football, making the national under-sixteen team. He was certainly a naturally gifted young man.

During a trip to see family on the Gold Coast, Paul decided to send a short video of his son's touch rugby highlights to a local club, which passed it on to the New Zealand Warriors. They offered him a contract within days.

Watching this skinny kid make a fool of plenty of other talented touch footy players is spellbinding. His footwork could have easily been out of a dance production, where he was the main act. Then there were the long, flat passes that hit their intended recipients easily. This young player had no interest in watching David Copperfield or David Blain, but he certainly had the skills of a magician on a sporting field.

Johnson continued to impress, progressing through the ranks, from Junior Warriors and Junior Kiwis to full first-grade debut in 2011.

It was during his first year of first grade that he really showed all his prodigious talent, during the preliminary final against the Melbourne Storm at AAMI Park. The prize: an NRL grand final berth. The Warriors led by two with less than four minutes to go. Johnson received the ball in centre field, about fifteen metres out from Melbourne's goal-line. He shaped to pass to his teammates as he ran across the field, drawing in defenders until a hole opened up, then offloaded to Lewis Brown to score. This was supposed to be a boy playing against men, but Johnson had enough confidence and skill to upstage many veterans that day. He'd just turned twenty-one.

Johnson's debuted for the Kiwis the next year, a match memorable mainly for his eighty-metre runaway intercept try. So, with high hopes, it was on to the World Cup in 2013. He didn't have his best game early in the semi-final, struggling to execute his kicks effectively. England's defence certainly contained the young halfback, stifling his time and space. Yet sport can turn on its head in a split second. A single decision can mean winning or losing.

England's first mistake happened with sixty seconds left until full-time. The Kiwis had time for one set of tackles as they spread it wide, finding space and driving past halfway. Sonny Bill Williams shuffled then charged into the English defensive line on the second-to-last tackle, a rather innocuous-looking play. Things then happened a little in slow motion. Blame the fatigue or Williams' ability to attract defenders like locusts, but George Burgess made the wrong decision and caught the Kiwi across the face with his arm. Penalty. Six more tackles.

'Ohhh noooooooo!!!' Jonathan Davies screamed in horror from the BBC television commentary box. Blinding bias at the moment aside, the theatrics on the field and the passion of those behind the microphones added to what was an astonishing moment in the game. It was equal parts comedy and drama, whether watching at 3am on Sunday in Auckland or during the cool Saturday afternoon in London. You couldn't leave your seat.

The Kiwis opted for a quick tap. Three tackles in, Issac Luke was stopped inches from England's line, with prop Frank Paul-Nu'uausala at dummy half. The big forward flung a long, high pass out to his halfback, who took it miraculously above his head. Kevin Sinfield, with thirteen years' experience at international level, must have missed watching Johnson's touch highlights as he rushed out of the line, hoping to put pressure and stop the Kiwi halfback.

Shaun Johnson's reaction at scoring the winning try, on the last play, in the last seconds of the semi-final. RLPhotos.com

But Johnson used this opportunity to swerve around his opposite. Sinfield missed and Johnson strolled past, leaving the England captain dazed, then dived over to score, breaking every English heart at the same time.

Paul Johnson remembered thinking his son was about to do something special as time slowly wound up:

> I looked at the clock with twenty seconds to go and had
> a gut feeling Shaun was going to pull one out of the hat.
> When he scored it was exactly as I thought. Although,
> in saying that, I stood there like a stunned mullet taking
> in what I had just seen. The following kick was to win
> the game, the kick goes over and it was at that point I
> jumped for joy and cried like a baby.

During a newspaper interview when he was thirteen, Shaun told an amazed reporter that all he wanted to do was to play rugby league for the Warriors and for the Kiwis. He only had to wait ten years to achieve both and turn his childhood dream into reality, with his dad in the stands to watch it happen.

Heartache and revenge

Although Steve McNamara was on the losing side that afternoon, and as the reality of losing a semi-final in the last few seconds started to hit home, he realised the part he had played in what was one of rugby league's best ever games.

'This World Cup, this occasion and many others throughout the tournament have done tremendous things for our sport. I'm privileged to be part of it, with 60,000–70,000 people, at our national stadium supporting rugby league.'

No one could begrudge or criticise England's performance. Rugby league's administrators could cherish a breathtaking example of the sport in London. Australia put in a master-class of rugby league a week later in the final, easily beating New Zealand 34–2. The fact that it was between two neutral countries didn't dampen enthusiasm for the occasion, though, as a world record crowd of 74,468 packed out the magnificent Old Trafford ground.

Revenge would come swiftly for England and New Zealand. The Kiwis avenged their World Cup final loss by winning the 2014 Four Nations, plus they strung together three wins against the Kangaroos for the first time in more than fifty years. England managed a 2–1 series victory against New Zealand in November of 2015, reclaiming some of their strut at the same time.

Australia claimed the 2016 Four Nations with ease. Mal Meninga looms as the key to restoring Kangaroo dominance. Will the emerging nations like France, Samoa, Fiji and Tonga be as competitive in 2017? That is up for debate. If the entertainment is anything like the 2013 event, it will make for tremendous viewing. It's an endeavour that must continue to be nurtured, built upon and celebrated.

Scoreboard: **New Zealand 20** (Roger Tuivasa-Sheck 2, Shaun Johnson tries; Shaun Johnson 4 goals) defeated **England 18** (Sean O'Loughlin, Kallum Watkins, Sam Burgess tries; Kevin Sinfield 3 goals). Attendance: 67,545.

ACKNOWLEDGEMENTS

I have many people to thank for helping put this book together.

Firstly, thank you to the superb team at ABC Books/ HarperCollins. Helen Littleton, who encouraged and guided me from start to finish, a special thank you. To Brigitta Doyle, Lachlan McLaine, Matt Howard and Georgia Williams, thanks for all your hard work too. It's such a team effort and everyone's contribution made it possible.

To Brad Fittler and Shaun Johnson, thanks for allowing us to use your photos on the cover.

Throughout the last two years, I've been struck at how genuine rugby league people are. Thank you to everyone I've interviewed for their time. This includes Anthony Field, Brett Kimmorley, Brian and Mike McClennan, Clive Griffiths, Chris Rattue, Dean Bell, Frank Endacott, Gary Parcell, Gary Kemble, Gavin Willacy, Gene Ngamu, Glenn Lazarus, David Niu, John Tamihere, Johnny Whiteley, Marc Ellis, Maurice Lindsay, Mark Harris, Mick Cronin, Nathan Fien, Nathan Cayless, Neal Coupland, Nigel Wood, Paul Johnson, Ray Haffenden, Richie Blackmore, Ricky Stuart,

Roy Christian, Sally Bolton, Shaun Edwards, Steve Gillis, Sir Rodney Walker, Tony Collins, Thomas Bosc, Tim Brasher, Steven Johnson, Wayne Pearce and Wally Lewis.

A big thank you to Wayne Bennett and Wally for writing a foreword and endorsement of the book.

To David Williams (RL Photos), Harry Edgar (RL Journal), Andrew Cornaga (Photosport), Rachel Kelly and Nigel Naseby (NRL Photos), I appreciate your assistance in bringing together a range of wonderful photos. Thanks to Clive for sharing his photo, plus Robert Gate for the helpful advice. Kathryn Hughes and Brigid Power from the Bradford Bulls Foundation – I appreciated your efforts also. Geoff Smith and Rod Wright – you guys helped greatly with past players.

To Debbie Golvan: you helped me make it happen, so a big thanks to you and all your guidance. Finally, to my family: thanks to Mum and Dad for your encouragement. And to Cherry, thanks for all your support throughout the last three years of writing, plus your willingness to play the role of sub-editor too.

BIBLIOGRAPHY

Tony Adams, *Masters of the Game: The Coaches Who Shaped Rugby League*. Ironbark, Sydney, 1996.

Malcolm Andrews, *The ABC of Rugby League*. ABC Books, Sydney, 2006.

Malcolm Andrews, *Rugby League Heroes*. Horwitz, Cammeray, NSW, 1982.

Eric Ashton and Ray French, *Glory in the Centre Spot*. Scratching Shed Publishing Ltd, Leeds, 2009.

Maurice Bamford, *A Touch of Class: The Frank Myler Story*. Cromwell Press Group, Trowbridge, 2010.

Dean Bell, *The Ultimate Warrior: The Dean Bell Story*. Gollancz, London, 1995.

Wayne Bennett and Steve Crawley, *Don't die with the music in you*. ABC Books, Sydney, 2002.

Wayne Bennett and Steve Crawley, *Wayne Bennett: The Man in the Mirror*. ABC Books, Sydney, 2008.

John Bloomfield, *Australia's sporting success: the inside story*. UNSW Press, Sydney, 2003.

Lee Briers with Mike Appleton, *Off the Cuff: The Lee Briers Autobiography*. Vertical Editions, Skipton, N.S.W, 2013.

Louis Bonnery, *Le rugby à XII le plus français du monde*. Cano & Franck, Limoux, 1996.

Neil Cadigan, *Rugby League Yarns*. Dolphin Press, Lane Cove, NSW, 2008.

John Cain, *BBC: 70 Years of Broadcasting*. British Broadcasting Corporation, London, 1992.

Phil Caplan, *Shoey the Lionheart: The Mick Shoebottom Story*. Tempus Publishing, Gloucestershire, 2004.

Stanley Chadwick, *Kangaroo Tours: The Story of the Australian Rugby League Visits to England*. Venturers Press, Huddersfield, 1948.

Clive Churchill, *They Called Me the Little Master: Clive Churchill's Colourful Story as Told to Jim Mathers; An Autobiography by the Famous Australian Rugby League International*. Percival, Sydney, 1962.

Terry Clawson and Steve Truelove, *All the Wrong Moves*. The Book Factory, Dewsbury, 1990.

Ian Collis and Alan Whiticker, *100 Years of Rugby League*. New Holland Publishers Australia, Chatswood, NSW, 2007.

Ian Collis and Alan Whiticker, *Rugby League through the Decades: All the Players, All the Statistics – Everything that's Happened in Rugby League since 1907*. New Holland Publishers, Chatswood, 2011.

Mike Colman, *Super League: The Inside Story*. Pan Macmillan, Sydney, 1996.

Alan Clarkson, *Meninga: My Life in Football*. HarperSports, Pymble, NSW, 1995.

John Coffey and Bernie Wood, *The Kiwis: 100 Years of International Rugby League*. Hodder Moa, Auckland, 2007.

Richard de la Riviere, *Rugby League, a Critical History 1980–2013*. League Publications Ltd, Brighouse, 2013.

Philip Dine, *French Rugby Football: A Cultural History*. Berg, Oxford, 2001.

Helen Elward and Graeme Langlands, *Billy Smith: A Saint From Head to Toe*. Best Legenz, Wentworthville, NSW, 2004.

Gary Freeman and Richard Becht, *Tiger Tiger Kiwi Rooster: the Gary Freeman story*. Moa Beckett, Auckland, 1992.

Ray French, *The Rugby League Lions: Australia and New Zealand*. Faber & Faber, London, 1985.

Henri Garcia, *Champagne Rugby: The Golden Age of French Rugby League*. London League Publications, London, 2007.

Angus Gillies, *Matthew Ridge: Take No Prisoners*. Hodder Moa Beckett, Auckland, 1998.

Mark Graham, *Mark My Words: The Mark Graham Story*. The Sporting Press, Auckland, 1989.

Geoff Greenwood, *Australian Rugby League's Greatest Games*. Murray, Sydney, 1978.

John Harms, *The Pearl: Steve Renouf's Story*. University of Queensland Press, St Lucia, 2005.

Iestyn Harris, *There and back: my journey from league to union and back again*. Mainstream Publishing, Edinburgh, 2005.

Glenn Jackson, *Benji, Benji Marshall: My Game, My Story*. Hachette, Sydney, 2011.

Paul Kimmage, *Full Time: The Secret Life of Tony Cascarino*. Simon & Schuster, London, 2000.

Adrian McGregor, *Simply the Best: The 1990 Kangaroos*. University of Queensland Press, St Lucia, 1991.

Keith Macklin, *History of Rugby League Football*. Paul, London, 1974.

John Matheson. *Stacey Jones: Keeping the Faith*. Hodder Moa Beckett, Auckland, 2002.

Steve Menzies with Norman Tasker, *Beaver: the Steve Menzies story*. Allen & Unwin, Crows Nest, 2008.

David Middleton, *Rugby League Week's Green and Gold Heroes – 80 Years of International Football*. Australian Consolidated Press, Sydney, 1989.

Martin Offiah with David Lawrenson, *Offiah: My Autobiography*. CollinsWillow, London, 1997.

Frank Perrin, *Rugby à XIII, Un Rugby de Defi*. Par The Book, Lille, 2011.

Bernard Pratviel, *Immortel Pipette*. Editions Empreinte, Cedex, 2012.

Johnny Raper with Alan Clarkson, *The Man in the Bowler Hat: Johnny Raper's Tearaway Life*. Ironbark, Chippendale, NSW, 1997.

Rugby League of Legends: 100 Years of Rugby League in Australia. National Museum of Australia, Canberra, 2008.

Rugby League World Cup 2000: Official Souvenir. Programme Publications Group, Liverpool 2000.

Rugby League World Cup series 1954: Official Souvenir. Rugby Football League, Leeds, 1954.

Mike Rylance, *The Forbidden Game: The Untold Story of French Rugby League*. League Publications Ltd, Brighouse, 2011.

Mike Stephenson, *Stevo: Looking Back*. Vertical, Skipton, 2007.

Gorden Tallis with Mike Coleman. *Raging Bull*. Pan Macmillan, Sydney, 2003.

Kevin Walters, *Brave Hearts*. Pan Macmillan Australia, Sydney, 1999.

Alan Whiticker, *Rugby League Test Matches in Australia*. ABC Books, Sydney, 1994.

Alan Whiticker, *Captaining the Kangaroos*. New Holland, Frenchs Forest, NSW, 2004.

Alan Whiticker, *Mud, Blood and Beer: Rugby League in the 1970s*. New Holland Publishing, Chatswood, NSW, 2014.

Alan Whiticker and Ian Collis, *The Top 10 of Rugby League*. New Holland Publishing, Chatswood, NSW, 2010.

Alan Whiticker and Ian Collis, *101 Great Rugby League Players*. New Holland Publishing, Chatswood, NSW, 2012.

Alan Whiticker and Glen Hudson, *The Encyclopedia of Rugby League Players*. Gary Allen, Wetherill Park, NSW, 2007.

Ruben Wiki with Richard Becht. *Ruben Wiki*. Hachette, Auckland, 2006.

Gavin Willacy, *Rugby League Bravehearts: The Official History of Scottish Rugby League*. London League Publications Ltd, London, 2002.

Periodicals and magazines

2008 Rugby League World Cup Program: The Final. Martin Lenehan and Mark Cashman. ACP Men's Lifestyle, Sydney, 2008.

Best of Rugby League Week: Our First 20 Years. Australian Consolidated Press, Sydney, 1989.

Halifax Rugby League Centenary World Cup. Big Tours Limited, Wembley, 1995.

L'Australienne Kangaroos versus Angleterre: Stade Pershing 31 decembre. William Walker & Sons, Otley, 1933.

Rugby League News. Vol. 1, no. 1, May 1920–73. NSW Rugby Football League, Sydney.

Rugby League Week. Vol. 1, no.1 1970–72 vol. 31, no. 33, 2000. Modern Magazines, Sydney.

Rugby League World Cup 1988 Final Souvenir Program. New Zealand Breweries for the New Zealand Rugby Football League, 1988.

Rugby League World Cup 2000 Final Program. Rugby Football World Cup 2000 Limited, 2000.

Rugby League World Cup 2013 Semi-final 1 Program. ProgrammeMaster, 2013.

Rugby League, Stones Bitter World Cup Final: Australia v Great Britain: Official Programme: Saturday 24 October 1992. David Howes. Wembley Stadium, Wembley, 1992.

Souvenir of the Australian Rugby League Kangaroo's World Tour 1933–34. William Walker & Sons, Otley, 1933.

World Cup Series 1960. Rugby Football League, Electric Press. 1960.

World Cup Series 1970: Great Britain v. Australia. Rugby Football League, Regent, Leeds, 1970.

DVDs and other media

Slammin' Sam. Fox Sports, 2013.

Joey: The Andrew Johns: The Story So Far. Sony Music, 2002.

Pride of the Lions: 100 Years of British Rugby League. PDI Media, 2008.

Rugby League's Greatest Tries and Greatest Players DVD. Visual Entertainment Group, 2009.

Rugby League World Cup: Australia 2008, The Final. Visual Entertainment Group, 2008.

Sportsworld. George Rainey interview, ID 4535. Radio New Zealand Collection, *Ngā Taonga Sound & Vision,* 6 November 1988.

Super League Super Men. Sky Sports, 2012.

Story of Rugby League DVD. BNT Productions, 2003.

Newspapers

The Daily Express

The Daily Mirror

The Daily Telegraph

The Guardian

Herald Sun

The Independent

The Mail

New Zealand Herald

The Sydney Morning Herald

The Times

The New York Times

Yorkshire Post

Websites

BBC.co.uk

Fox Sports, www.foxsports.com.au

The Guardian UK, www.theguardian.com/uk

Rugby League DVDs, www.rugbyleaguedvds.com

Rugby League Project, www.rugbyleagueproject.org

THEIR
FINEST
HOUR

THEIR FINEST HOUR

A HISTORY OF THE RUGBY LEAGUE WORLD CUP IN 10 MATCHES

ANDREW MARMONT

ABC
Books

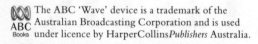 The ABC 'Wave' device is a trademark of the
Australian Broadcasting Corporation and is used
under licence by HarperCollins*Publishers* Australia.

First published in Australia in 2017
by HarperCollins*Publishers* Australia Pty Limited
ABN 36 009 913 517
harpercollins.com.au

HarperCollins*Publishers*
Level 13, 201 Elizabeth Street, Sydney NSW 2000, Australia
Unit D1, 63 Apollo Drive, Rosedale, Auckland 0632, New Zealand
A 53, Sector 57, Noida, UP, India
1 London Bridge Street, London, SE1 9GF, United Kingdom
2 Bloor Street East, 20th floor, Toronto, Ontario M4W 1A8, Canada
195 Broadway, New York NY 10007, USA

National Library of Australia Cataloguing-in-Publication data:

Marmont, Andrew, author.
  Their finest hour: a history of the Rugby League World Cup
  in 10 matches / Andrew Marmont.
  978 0 7333 3587 7 (paperback)
  978 1 4607 0506 3 (ebook)
  Rugby League football – History.
  Rugby League football – Tournaments – History.
  Rugby League football players.
  World Cup (Rugby football)

Cover design by Luke Causby, Blue Cork
Cover images: Brad Fittler © National Rugby League;
Shaun Johnson © National Rugby League;
Puig Aubert by Universal/Corbis/VCG via Getty Images;
Typeset in Bembo Std by Kirby Jones
Printed and bound in Australia by McPhersons Printing Group
The papers used by HarperCollins in the manufacture of this book are a natural,
recyclable product made from wood grown in sustainable plantation forests.
The fibre source and manufacturing processes meet recognised international
environmental standards, and carry certification.

To Bobo and Grandpa,
for encouraging me to chase my dreams.